I0149650

I'm Such a Tourist

I'm Such A Tourist

First Edition Printing

ISBN: 978-0-692-70421-9

1. Title 2. Author 3. Travel & Tourism

I'm Such a Tourist

Ali Al-Naama

Preface

My name is Ali Al-Naama, and I am Qatari. I was born and raised in Doha, but was fortunate enough to see the world as a young man, having grown up in a family that valued travel as an essential part of life. This later led me to study in both Qatar and Leeuwarden, the Netherlands at Stenden University of Applied Sciences; at the same time, I continued my exploration of the world. I come from a family that was fundamental to the journalism industry in Qatar. My grandfather lit the initial spark by establishing the first newspaper in the country. I remember visiting his office when I was a child, where I was always fascinated by his work ethics, his personality, his creativity, and his way of thinking, all of which have guided me to where I am today.

I was lucky in that my parents always advocated for me to pursue what I aspired to in life, and instilled in me that nothing is impossible. The first time I felt I didn't belong was when I got into law school. Even then, when I was completely lost, they urged me not to settle for a life that was not true to myself. So I didn't. I changed my major to study Business Administration with an emphasis in International Tourism Management and that is when I found myself. I remember attending the first class, Introduction to the Tourism Industry, and feeling a passion for something for the first time in my life. That is when I fell in love with tourism.

By my second year, I already had a vision of writing a tourism book. I knew I didn't want it to be like any other schoolbook; I wanted it to be interesting! This passion I had ignited for this subject kept my focus on the book. I truly wanted to become an integral part of the sector, and write a book that would provide awareness and education and arouse curiosity about the tourism sector. I found the information provided about the tourism sector to be incomplete and lacking a full picture, creating an underrated view of the travel and tourism industry. I knew I wanted to change that.

In order to share my passion and entice the reader, I decided to create an interactive story about tourism that would not only inform the reader, but invite him or her into the driver's seat. By awakening and addressing the tourist in every reader, I would be able to present pertinent information about the sector, and appeal to a larger audience. So by presenting a book that immediately involved the reader, I now had the ability to explain all of the moving parts of the industry, including agendas of both the tourist and the tourism industry as well as a view from the global economic standpoint.

Tourism is much more than just a topic about travel. It is about destinations built on showcasing cultures and traditions of local communities. It is about the astronauts that have traveled beyond our atmosphere for exploration and curiosity. It is about a sector that has struggled and evolved over time, parallel to the advancements in technology. The sector has taken its place as one of the top in the world, and is predicted to be the number-one sector of our future. It is an industry that elicits respect, encourages creativity, and shares knowledge.

DEDICATION

Aisha Hussein El Chami, 1938-2003

VISA
APPROVED
IMMIGRATION THAILAND
8 JAN 2013
DEPARTED
INTERNATIONAL
TRAVEL
PASS FREE
IMMIGRATION
DEPARTED
10 DEC 2015
LONDON
ARRIVED
20 FEB 2015
DATE OF
ISSUE
FIRST

Acknowledgements

I want to thank my parents and brothers for the memories we created as a family traveling around the world, and for making that a family tradition ever since we were little kids. This was the seed that grew into my passion for tourism and loving this industry.

I want to thank my best friend, Mohammed Al-Jarman, for guiding and advising me, for making me discover tourism, and believing that my passion for tourism is special. Special thanks goes to Shaikha Al-Mudahka, Fatma Al-Mulla, and Aisha Al-Khamees for being part of my tourism experience from the very beginning. You all encouraged me to go ahead with the book, and I thank you for helping me shape its direction. I am so happy with the outcome. Thank you for the inspiration, "Hatters.

Professionally speaking, I would like to thank the tourism management faculty in Stenden University Qatar. I learned so much from every lecturer, and they made me grow professionally. I want to thank also Mohammed Suleiman, my colleague and friend, for his constant support and help.

"We keep moving forward, opening new doors, and doing new things, because we're curious…and curiosity keeps leading us down new paths."

–Walt Disney

VISA
APPROVED
IMMIGRATION THAILAND
8 JAN 2013
DEPARTED
INTERNATIONAL
TRAVEL
PASS FREE
IMMIGRATION
DEPARTED
10 DEC 2015
LONDON
FIRST
DATE OF
ISSUE
ARRIVED
20 FEB 2015

Part One
The Beginning of an Industry

Innovation is a new idea that expands the knowledge around a process or makes an idea or device more effective. It creates better solutions to once unsolvable situations. Innovation is original ideas that bring light to areas where there was once darkness. And mankind has been notable firmly as innovative since the first humans began to create tools. Their instincts led them to ignite the motivation for better, for more, and for different ways of life. They were the original innovators of humankind, sparking objects together to make fire, making tools to hunt and gather, and creating languages to communicate with one another. When innovation began to better lives, the tourism industry began stirring. It pushed humanity's creativity and motivation beyond its current status. People became aware that not only could they get from one place to another, but that they wanted to whether out of need to find food and shelter or bubbling curiosity that they could not express. The first step of mankind was the first of infinite steps for tourists.

The word *tourist* is defined as a person traveling to and staying in places outside his or her usual environment for [no less than one night and] not more than one consecutive year for leisure, business, and other purposes. This is the definition of a tourist by the United Nations World Tourism Organization (UNWTO), the agency accountable for the promotion of responsible, sustainable, and universally accessible tourism. Coined in 1772, the word originates from the word *tour* meaning a circle or movement around a central point or axis. Over time, the meaning has changed to represent "one's turn." By adding the suffix *-ist,* it suggests the action of moving in a circle. Describing a circle implies returning to one's starting point; a tour is a round-trip journey, the act of leaving and ultimately returning to the original starting point. One who takes such a journey can then be called a *tourist.*

Who *is* the tourist and why was mankind prompted to become tourists? The story of every person's travels is as diverse as the person. People go to various places for particular reasons, and want to see and do specific things. But the real push from the inside to travel, the motivation, is what connects all tourists together. This inherent need for travel started at the beginning of mankind. But what made our ancestors want to travel? What constituted the beginning of the tourism industry? To understand completely the present and future tourist, the journey of the past must first be absorbed.

Although the words *tourist* and *tourism* were not officially coined until the eighteenth century, humans have been traveling since the beginning of time. Even with the initial mode of transportation, walking on foot, people had reason to go from one place to another, as we do today. This first method of transportation, the human body, satisfied the needs of these first travelers. But their motivation was far from what we would consider a motivation to travel as a tourist today. They were migrating as part of a mission, a primal need. People left their home dwellings in search of food, water, shelter, salvation, or land. During these early times, they were presented with many physical challenges, some of which carried a high probability of death. Weather, illness, terrain, and needing food and shelter while traveling were all key factors, unlike the more relatively lavish concerns of the modern tourist.

The constant development of transportation has modified both the tourist and the tourism industry. As transportation has advanced, people have been able to get from one place to another quicker and relatively safer. One of the initial forms of travel besides that of walking were canoes crafted some 45,000 years ago. Humans then used them to find food and resources. This is the time when Neanderthals began hunting marine mammals as well, and from there, maritime trading grew in sync with the monsoon winds, resulting in water travels for trade that was remarkably quicker, and allowed for further traveling, than land trade. The invention of water transport increased the mobility of man faster than any other previous attempt or invention. Water transport, first in handmade canoes, and later in larger ships, brought about the first transport of goods in bulk from one location to another: trade. This was one of the first big steps in transportation that directly affected the tourist and tourism industry.

Even before actual money was an idea, trade of items and bartering grew the roots of future tourism. One part of a city, nation, or country would have natural resources that other places did not. Some groups of people were inventing and crafting items of which other cultures had never heard. This is where the most basic idea of tourism started. These groups of people from different locations would travel to trade their natural and handmade goods for those of the visited location, then return home. This could be compared to the modern tourist who is motivated by shopping in other countries for items that cannot be found in his or her own country. But still, the core motivations of ancient peoples to travel set them apart from the modern definition of a tourist.

As the sea became increasingly prevalent for travel concerning trade, this era quickly led to a time of traveling for the sake of exploration. The domestication of animals as early as 9000 BC allowed for the hauling of objects too heavy to for people to physically transport to be moved from one place to another with ease. This later evolved to using animals such as horses for quicker transport of man himself. The drive of the traveler changed as well, from the need to travel for resources to the need to travel out of curiosity about far-off lands. Travelers involved with exploring did not always plan to return to their location of origin; again, this is a differentiating factor from the definition of the tourist today.

But was this surge in traveling the key to the beginning of tourism? When people traveled from their home to lands for resources or exploration, were they in fact taking part in their destination's eating, drinking, lodging, and cultural activities? Tourism, according to the UNWTO, is a social, cultural, and economic phenomenon which entails the movement of people to countries or places outside their usual environment for personal or business/professional purposes. These people are the tourists, and tourism has to do with their activities.

The story of the tourist and the growth of tourism happened with the natural flow of time. Centuries before we acknowledged the modern terms *tourist* and *tourism*, there were clear indications of both. Among them were the Babylonians and their development of currency, which sparked the onset of trade in 4000 BC that led to travel and the most definite example of tourism. Not only was this the invention of the idea of money, but individuals could now pay for transportation and accommodation. And in 2700 BC, the Egyptians started building elaborate pyramids that drew a considerable amount of visitors, people who journeyed there purely out of curiosity to see the monuments: tourists.

Stories like those of the Babylonians and Egyptians have been recorded all through time in every country. The concept of travels by people purely motivated by curiosity and pleasure, not just out of the necessity to fulfill primal needs, is not unique. For example, in 776 BC the citizens in Ancient Greece organized an athletic competition to honor the god Zeus that directly influenced the modern Olympic Games. This is one of the earliest examples of Sports Tourism, in which a sporting event in one location draws people to an event and area. The Phoenicians as well participated in catering to tourists as they carried paying passengers around the Mediterranean, laying the groundwork for what we identify today as tourist attractions, activities, and amenities.

The more modern explorers were a natural progression of the tourist as well, growing from a more advanced need to travel out of curiosity of the unknown, paired with the advancements in transportation and wealth. Voyagers like Chinese explorer Xu Fu who in the third century BC explored Japan; Greek explorer Euthymenes who explored the coast of West Africa in the sixth century BC; Persian Ahmad ibn Rustah who in the tenth century explored Russia, Scandinavia, and Arabia; and Venetian Marco Polo who explored China and the Mongol Empire in the thirteenth and fourteenth centuries. Were these adventurers merely explorers, or were they the tourists of their time? Not only were they traveling to discover new land and find better living conditions for themselves and their families, but also to survey other lands occupied with cultures outside their scope of understanding. Transportation innovations made it possible for these explorers to cover more land, or sea, faster and safer than via previous options. And as accessibility to travel grew, so did exploration.

The modern tourist, however, was not officially recognized or defined until more recent history, even though the recognition came after centuries of travelers, explorers, and historic tourists. With the emergence of travel writers, not traveling itself, one of the earliest known written records of travel purely in pursuit of pleasure was during the early fourteenth century. Petrarch's (1304-1374) writings of his ascent of Mount Ventoux, dated 1336, express his pleasure and intent to climb purely to see the view from the famous height. These travel writings showed his comparisons between climbing the mountain and his own moral progress in life. Then, during the tenth- to thirteenth-century Song dynasty, secular travel writers such as Su Shi (eleventh century) and Fan Chengda (twelfth century) become popular in China. Under the Ming dynasty, Xu Xiake continued this practice. And the Burgundian poet Michault Taillevent later composed his own horrified recollections of a 1430 trip through the Jura Mountains.

By the Middle Ages, Christianity, Buddhism, and Islam all had widespread traditions of pilgrimage that motivated even the lower classes to undertake distant journeys for health or spiritual improvement while seeing the sights along the way. Then there was the Grand tour, a traditional trip around Europe taken mainly by upper-class European young men of wealth. This custom started in 1660 and continued to flourish until the invention of large-scale rail transit in the 1840s. The tour served as an educational opportunity and rite of passage.

The next big steps in transportation were the steam engine and railroad system, followed closely by the steam ship, which sped up global transport and began holding passengers in the early 1800s.But it was the rail system that opened up the quicker possibilities of travel with relative ease and safety from one place to another with the intention of returning to one's home. Trains created a higher accessibility to travel to destinations purely out of leisure, never seen before in this magnitude. Tourists then were able to restfully sit and look out the windows of trains as they were taken to destinations for business or leisure. Yet still, in 1800, only 1% of the population could travel in a style we currently define as a vacation. Travel destinations were for the upper-class only. It was the privileged who could travel to distant parts of the world to see works of art, explore magnificent terrains, absorb new languages, experience new cultures, and taste different cuisines. For laborers, vacationing was still simply impossible.

At that time, train operations also started booking not only the train rides, but hotels for the tourists, creating a "package tour." Thomas Cook is credited with the creation of organized tours. In 1841, he chartered a train to take a group of campaigners from Leicester to a rally in Loughborough, an eleven-mile distance. By 1872, he had formed a business, Thomas Cook & Son that grew to become one of the largest and most well-known travel agents before being nationalized in 1948.

But the big breakthrough in the availability of travel to all classes did not come until the mid-twentieth century, with another surge in the transportation industry. The invention of the automobile clearly placed the freedom of transportation into the hands of the individual. Groups or families began to travel within their own countries via automobile or to nearby countries accessible by land. It wasn't until the invention and industry of the commercial airplane that far-distance travel became highly accessible in the early 1970s. This was also the first obtainable way to travel internationally with ease and at lightning-fast speeds, in comparison to sea travel. Still at a heavy cost to the traveler, but more accessible than it had ever been in the past, travel by airplanes changed the tourism market drastically.

So as one can see, the paths of the tourist and tourism from the beginning of time have flourished and dramatically changed. Man-made and natural forces have moved the progression along. Of course without the evolution of man, there would be no evolution of the industry. As discussed, many moving parts directly and indirectly influenced its progression. And as the world evolved, cities and countries formed, and the modern tourist emerged, as did modern tourism.

Cities and nations began their involvement in the tourism industry as they grew more aware of their natural and man-made treasures unique to their areas. During the time of heavy trade, often city authorities would help to ensure that visitors to their land not only enjoyed their stay and made their trades, but started to encourage them to spend their currency on local items and services. In order for tourism to thrive in a city, nation, or country, many working parts need to be balanced. The working part that most effected tourism in ancient times was accessibility, the transportation system required for people to visit their destination. And once there, accommodations, places for the people to find food and shelter, and, thirdly, attractions kept them there. People often traveled to see man-made attractions and natural attractions. This was their pull to a destination.

Today however, there are many moving parts of the tourism industry that must work together in order to keep it moving seamlessly. Not only does a destination need to be easily accessible through viable transportation, but the various accommodations and amenities rank high on a tourist's list of demands. The destination itself has to create some sort of appealing marketing information to reach the tourist initially.

There must also be attractions and/or activities that pull the tourist in, and almost always, the governing body of the destination is required for compliance in all aspects. Today, a large number of countries' economic survival is balanced on tourism. Tourism has a direct effect on the social, cultural, educational, and economic sectors of national societies and their international relations.

Although it did not emerge as an "industry" until modern times, just like the tourist, tourism began forming at the same time people started traveling. It has been the physical accessibility to travel, the things to see, the places to stay, and the monetary accessibility to travel that has changed. As for the tourist, although early motives to travel from one's home differ from our reasons now, we are finding that some of the bigger key motivators behind the desire to travel have not changed much over the centuries. The thinking of the tourist started as simple motivations to find the essential resources to live, and then progressed to exchanging one's territory's goods with those of others and return home. This advanced even further into the explorer, motivated by more than just primal needs, but also out of curiosity. And the traveler who sought out far lands to see monuments and unfathomable creations by man and nature, motivated by pleasure, has turned into today's tourist, full of curiosity and intent on finding pleasure and respite.

When we look deeper into the tourist of today, we find a complex circuit, the connections between emotions, motivations, and direct and indirect influences all pushing and pulling him or her to travel. The modern tourist has specific expectations of satisfaction when he or she travels, seamlessly woven together by inner and outer persuasions. Compared to the past tourist, the present tourist has the commonplace privilege of taking travel outside his or her home with easier accessibility, while the whole world is out there inviting him or her to experience what it has to offer.

Part Two
The Tourist Thinking

There are origins, a sparking ignition point, to every person's thoughts, actions, needs, and desires. An innate reason for doing things. The tourist has motivations, like all people do, when he or she is making choices and forming plans about travel. The emotions and motives go hand in hand with each other, often intermingling so seamlessly it is hard to tell which came first. These internal stimuli are accompanied by external forces, and both of these bounce back and forth with each other. Once the decision to travel has been made, the trip itself is arranged and all of the details are addressed before departure. Any expectations and desired explorations the tourist has are acknowledged in order to assess and help meet the goals of the trip. Sometimes the expectations for the trip are explored internally and not addressed directly until the trip begins. The tourist is incessantly evaluating his or her trip, often internally, piece by piece as well as on a whole, altering his or her constantly changing level of satisfaction which influences his or her ever-changing path.

The tourist is the essential part to tourism. Without the tourist, there would be no need for the tourism industry. Mankind has transformed over time, and so has the tourist. The way he or she lives, the way he or she thinks. Humans are evolving every minute, day, year, decade, and century. New thinking creates new inventions, new inventions influence new thinking, and this means the tourist's thinking is progressing too, pushing the industry to stretch and form. This chapter will take an in-depth look into how the modern tourist thinks, propelling an entire industry forward.

MOTIVATION

Motivation directs a person's decisions, and can even affect his or her behavior in entirety. Motives can be as simple as eating because we are hungry or wearing warm clothing because we are cold. And external forces can influence a person's emotions concerning his or her actions and motives to do things, whether the person is aware of these outside influences or not. Where there are motives, there are strong internal influences: emotions. With a combination of internal and external forces, seen and unseen, individual's motivations can regularly be irresistible to the mental and psychological self.

There are two types of motivation: intrinsic/internal and extrinsic/external. Internal inspirations push the tourist forward from the inside out and external motivations, like marketing, pull the tourist toward a specific location. Although these two motivations can be considered opposites, they are tightly linked together that seldom is there a way to pinpoint which came first, the drive and need of the tourist, or the pull and embedded idea from the direct and indirect ads of specific businesses in the tourism industry.

TYPES OF TOURIST MOTIVATIONS

Travel motivations have changed over time. Ancestors were pushed ahead by the primal needs of survival, then by the hunt for resources that expanded into trade and then formed the early explorer. The motivators that next emerged thrust our modern tourist forward still today, like curiosity and the fascination with the unknown. However, there are impetuses that are even more exclusive to our contemporary tourist.

The tourism industry focuses on pulling tourists to precise locations. But if it was not for the tourist's inner drives pushing him or her, the tourism business would have nothing around which to frame its marketing plans. Each individual tourist is the target audience, and keeping in mind that every person is unique, the tourism business tailors its plans to common groups of motivations. Motivation is the process that initiates, guides, and maintains goal-oriented behaviors. Simply, motivation is what causes us to act. These driving forces can be all encompassing, both rooting deep within the tourist's essence and apparent in every detail of his or her conscious path. The basic types of motivation steering tourists are physical, psychological, cultural, interpersonal, and personal development. Within these motivated travel intentions are the foundational pushes that move a tourist toward one destination over another.

PHYSICAL MOTIVATIONS

Physical motivations relate to the body and well-being. Tourists who are physically motivated are pulled in the direction of localities that promote rest and relaxation, and provide leisure environments. Leisure travel satisfies a tourist's need to escape from reality and rest his or her body and mind. Every culture differs, but in general, people focus more on their busy lives today and less on the inherent need for their physical and mental well-being. The sorts of recuperating trips desired by these tourists are characterized by staying in relatively nice hotels or resorts, usually near waterfront locations. Light-footed guided tours of the areas are also often popular attractions on lists of things to do. During these sorts of getaways, the tourist frequently indulges in all of the luxury resources such as taking taxis at any cost to get to where he or she wants to go. And most inclusive vacation destinations put the tourist in the position to eat at restaurants or through room service for every meal, without having to be bothered to prepare his or her own meals.

The leisure tourist also includes another type of tourist that is equally as motivated to find and indulge in leisure. As all things in life are relative, so is luxury. The other common leisure tourist is usually referred to as a backpacker. These tourists, still focusing completely on leisure activities, rest, and relaxation, travel in a different, more affordable, style. Simply because a person is seeking relaxation he or she cannot find in everyday life does not mean he or she has a large disposable income. In fact, there are more economical tourists today, which aids in making travel and holidays more accessible. This group will stay in hostels; cook its own food; and walk, take public transit, or rent bikes to get from one spot to another. Just as leisure-seeking as the first group, these tourists still visit the same locations as any luxury-motivated individual, but are mindful of their budget.

Physical motivations also concern those traveling outside of their home areas for medical treatments or sporting events. Medical treatments can be anything from dental work to plastic surgery, medically necessary treatments, or those that are considered cosmetic. People find that these medical treatments cost less in countries outside of their own or that the specialist in the field of their medical needs practices someplace around which they need to plan a trip. Purely motivated to obtain medical treatment, these tourists travel in styles ranging from frugal to lavish, depending on the individual. These tourists are also often required to stay in or nearby the medical facility where the treatment was provided for safety reasons for a certain amount of time, extending their trips beyond receiving the medical services they required.

Sporting events call tourists as well. These travelers, depending on their fanaticism and investment in a sport, will become tourists within their own country when traveling to see a local team or possibly propel themselves all the way around the world for an event. Sporting events vary in type and size on many levels. The sports tourist can also fall on a spectrum just as varied. Some people love to support their local teams, others have pure enjoyment in watching sports at leisure, others have previously played the sport themselves at a local or even professional level, and there are those who simply wish to play the sport. Sport gamblers who enjoy betting on sporting events can also be identified as sports tourists, as well as those traveling to enjoy a destination sport themselves, such as surfing or skiing.

The other type of tourist in this category is one seeking physical enhancement. For example, people often travel to other countries for physical "boot camps." When wanting to get into shape, most people find it easier to take themselves completely out of their daily routine and travel to a destination where others are also seeking pure physical enhancement as well, typically guided by a trainer or teacher. These camps, or programs, sometimes include activities such as kickboxing, weight lifting, yoga, or running.

PSYCHOLOGICAL MOTIVATIONS

The second main type of tourist motivation is psychological. This means that the tourist is driven by things related to his or her mental and emotional state. All tourists, regardless of their principal motivation to travel, are strongly connected to their emotions. But this particular type of tourist is entirely driven by his or her emotions. Time and again these people travel because of nostalgia, romance, fantasy, adventure, and spirituality. The strongest of these emotional motivators is romance. Holidays that are intended for people to find, enhance, or save romance are one of the top reasons for travel in the industry. People traveling for romantic escapes plan trips that range from leisure to active based on the unique preferences of the individuals. There are also those who are not looking for love, but would like to make their current relationships stronger. Many couples travel together to romantic retreats in attempts to rekindle what has been lost in their relationships. And still there are those who travel to celebrate the love they have with their partners. These tourists plan travels together to various types of destinations purely to enjoy each other's company while doing things they both enjoy. Leisure is at the top of the lists these people make for what they're looking for when they travel.

Another psychological motivation for people to travel is nostalgia. Nostalgia affects almost everybody. Those who are wanting to re-create times in their lives, possibly a prior trip or previous living location, book trips back to those spots in hopes that they will be able to experience the same emotional connection as they did when they were there before. Unfortunately, nostalgia often creates false expectations for emotions that cannot be revisited identically to when they happened originally. Whether trips taken because of nostalgia satisfy the tourists as planned or not, many outside factors make these trips what they are. The original trips could have created lasting positive memories because of the people who had been there previously, who the tourists were as people during those times, and the states of the physical locations during the original travels. But not all of those factors can be re-created when returning, which may or may not cause dissatisfaction within the tourists.

Adventure travel is for the tourist seeking an emotional, and often physical, state often characterized as a "rush." At first glance, it would seem the adventure tourist is motivated by a physical motive. But fundamentally, it is the psychological surge that motivates him or her to pursue adventure tourism. The physical acts that he or she pursues are often somewhere on the scale of dangerous activities. Activities may include mountaineering, trekking, bungee jumping, mountain biking, canoeing, rafting, zip-lining, paragliding, or rock climbing. The motivation to travel to live out a fantasy, however, often presents things that are not exactly what they seem. But this is truly why one seeks out this type of vacation. The tourist is motivated by a search for a fantasy, surrounding one's self in an environment of things that are impossible, or improbable, in one's current life. On a certain level, tourists motivated by fantasy are similar to those motivated by the physical need to travel for leisure, and even other types of travel. Both are looking for an environment that lets them escape from their mundane lives and enjoy an almost-alternate reality for a period of time.

As times have changed, so have motivations. Curiosity as a motivation has been dulled down by the inundating abundance and oversaturated marketing industry. The ads people see in print and online are often overwhelming. Even if a person is one of the few who can resist clicking on an attractive picture of a beach resort on the outskirt of a jungle, he or she is still unknowingly seeing the ads, the pictures, and the pull from advertisements. So while a majority of vacations are being presented with a high level of fantasy attraction, the fantasy traveler is actually purposefully seeking out an atmosphere deliberately altered to provide a seamless fantasy experience.

Psychologically motivated tourists also include those traveling for spiritual reasons. Sometimes these tourists are traveling to other regions with which they share similar spiritual beliefs. Others also find that travel in itself is a spiritual journey, and select destinations they feel would enhance their time there not only physically, but spiritually. And there are also those who travel to find what inspires them. They may not have a particular spiritual definition for themselves, but are eager to take in, learn about, and experience firsthand all of the different ways other cultures experience and define spirituality in hopes that they too can embrace it and return home with a new inspiration.

CULTURAL MOTIVATIONS

The motivation for cultural travel is one that has stirred the tourist to go for centuries from his or her home to another place with the curiosity to explore. Cultural tourism is the top modern type of travel. The current tourist travels to experience other cultures regularly; this often comes up in many different types of vacations. Even with the flooding of technology into our lives that brings the awareness of far-off places to us via music, movies, and television, nothing brings these tourists closer to those cultures than putting themselves right in the middle of their desired environments. It is the lifestyle of the people in those geographical areas; the history of those people; and their art, architecture, religion(s), and other elements that helps shape their way of life that intoxicates this tourist. And there are endless options for the tourist motivated by culture. In some areas, one can find dozens of different types of cultures within a close distance of one's own home. One is then able to satisfy one's need to enlighten oneself with soaking up the culture of people firsthand by traveling outside one's home. Even though the journey of exploration thrives on the differences of other cultures, the often-found similarities between the new culture and one's own can be exhilarating as well. To find out that these often-mesmerizing communities could be linked to one's own is satisfying. One is then able to identify more closely with the cultures, and bring home a part of what they experience.

There are many smaller categories, and motives, of cultural travel such as specific focuses on art, music, literature, food, or history that drive the tourist. For example, there are tourists who travel precisely in search of exploring the art of a particular culture. While they visit their desired destinations, their driving motivation is to take in the sites focusing on the art of the culture. This could vary in all of the many media in which art is created and where it is located in a city or country. Similarly, there are those tourists who thrive on food, or specific cuisines of a region. These tourists fall into the specific category of culinary, or food, tourism. The motivator behind these tourists is the exploration of food. They pick locations to visit based on the food they want to experience. And often within any region, there could be endless options of different foods to try. Sometimes tourists of this nature will take classes on how to prepare foods of a region for enjoyment, and to bring back and share the knowledge with their home areas. Although food exploration is now a vital part of any cultural vacation, these tourists are using it as their main focus of travel.

Cultural travel has increased dramatically over the years. Again, because of the accessibility to travel around the world, cultural tourism is surging. Decades ago, the ability to directly place oneself in the middle of another region, country, or culture was almost unimaginable by most. But now, with options to travel abroad available for those with various budgets, tourists are able to experience a life outside of their own in person. The pure excitement and depth of curiosity stimulates this tourist, often time and time again on many, many travels.

INTERPERSONAL MOTIVATIONS

Interpersonal means that the motivation comes from a strong or close relationship with, or need for, another person or group of people, ranging from family and friends to business relationships to romantic involvements. In other words, this is the social tourist. The relationships this tourist has, or is seeking through travel, can be brief engagements lasting only the length of their travels, to lifelong relationships. Tourists can have more than one motivation, but typically, there is one motivation stronger than others when pushing a person to initiate a trip. For instance, a person may want to take a trip to see friends who live in another country he or she has wanted to visit. This trip could be motivated by an interpersonal motivation to see the friends, but also a physical motivation if the friends live in a location that intrigues this person. So which motivation would drive him or her? The island paradise to which his or her friends just moved, or the need to fulfill a longing to see lifelong friends? One motive always comes first. Although the trip may satisfy both needs, in terms of tourist motivation, there is always that first spark that inspires the journey.

Interpersonal travels mostly refer to the motivation to visit family, as well as close friends. This type of travel is one of the most common. Although family and friends may live halfway around the world, they may also live in closer proximity to the tourist, possibly requiring only a short flight or drive. The only reason that some may not see visiting family as a vacation is because often people associate vacation with leisure, adventure, or romance. Visiting family may not be the ideal getaway for all, but it is still one of the more common reasons people travel. It can also be one of the more economical ways to travel, being that often enough tourists traveling to see family and friends frequently board and eat with them. Depending on the individual, and sometimes the family, the tourists may choose an accommodation nearby. Again, choices vary based on preferences.

Overall, interpersonally motivated tourists are traveling out of a social necessity. Whether they want to visit family and friends or they are eager to escape from their daily lives, routines, families, or work. They do not necessarily demand leisure, culture, or fantasy, but they do want to share their time with others. Tourists travel by themselves even when they are seeking social getaways. Those brave enough to take on the world by themselves, and also the ones most eager to meet other people in the destinations at which they spend time, are motivated to make new friends.

PERSONAL DEVELOPMENT MOTIVATIONS

The last type of motivation for a tourist is personal development. Personal development is not limited to self-help, but includes development at the personal and professional levels. It embraces activities that improve awareness and identity, develop talents and potential, build human capital and facilitate employability, enhance quality of life, and contribute to the realization of dreams and aspirations. People motivated by this development often fall into a few general categories as to why they travel: for business, to attend classes or seminars, to pursue hobbies, or to increase their own personal development.

Business travel refers to those who are required to travel to an area outside of their homes for work-related reasons. Often, business travel is scheduled for these tourists to meet with colleagues in their company or similar ones, meet with clients, or attend conventions and exhibitions. The core motivation of these tourists is to perform work. Some individuals also travel to attend classes or seminars. These endeavors are not always mandated by an employer, but can often be supplemental to one's employment or enhancing skills that could be of use not only to one's employer but to the individual, either for current use or to aide in future employability. When these tourists take on personal travels for classes, it is because they want to gain better work skills overall to increase their performance and maintain a competitive edge in their fields currently and for the future.

Personal development can also motivate people to expand their personal skills. For example, sometimes people travel outside their regions to learn more about their hobbies, and to explore their hobbies in depth in other cultures. Others want to gain new hobbies, explore the options of activities that might pique their interests, or create new hobbies. Having enjoyable hobbies and activities to supplement one's life is important to this tourist. If he or she does not feel he or she can make the time to attain these things in daily life, he or she seeks a travel destination to fulfill this need, in hopes of carry on with this hobby after returning home.

Personal development motivations can encompass self-help. Self-help comes in many different forms. Tourists often find destinations that can help them focus on their inner selves, the opposite of tourists focused solely on their physical selves. Finding self-help is unique for each and every person. But common themes include seeking an emotional and spiritual support for an illness; attaining a stronger sense of self, including beliefs, strengths, and weaknesses; or singularly focusing on a personal issue he or she is unable to successfully explore in daily life. A lot of people strive to be better people and understand how they feel. These tourists are motivated to find ways and places that can enhance their inner selves, and teach them skills they can use in their daily lives. Often when traveling far from home, people are able to concentrate fully on tasks or skills, and they feel supported in going home again knowing they have the ability to maintain an inner level of the life skills they focused on in depth while traveling.

TOURIST INFLUENCE

There are clear reasons why a person is internally motivated to travel. They have been narrowed down to five types of intrinsic motivations that push people forward. But the tourist is influenced to travel by external factors as well. Push factors are what aid in forcing a person to travel away from his or her current region. But pull factors are what draw people away from one place to a new location. This push/pull factor can be seen in all areas of life. One example is supply and demand. Do people buy more because something is so bountiful? Or do companies create more because of the demand from consumers? This conversation could be eternal, and has been going on for centuries. The same could be said of the tourist and the motivations to travel. Do people travel to a destination because they are pushed by internal motivations, or do they travel because they are pulled there by the tourism industry? Again, it's hard to tell what comes first. And in almost all cases, it is examined as a continuum. Without the tourist, of course there would be no tourism industry. This is not the debate. The question is *why* is the tourist traveling? Specialists in tourism have basically agreed on the answer. Both. Tourists travel because of a combination of internal and external motivations, a combination of push *and* pull.

TYPES OF PULL MOTIVATIONS

There are a few basic pull motivators: physical pulls, pulls from the tourism industry, and consumerism. Physical pulls are just that, physical. So the tourist pulled in by this enticement would be attracted to the natural beauty of a destination. Pulls from the tourism industry are not at a loss, with direct and indirect organized marketing. And consumerism binds them together by helping to explain and answer the questions of why we travel in the first place. All three can be directly related to one another, but to really understand how all of the pieces work together, it is easier to look at them individually first.

PHYSICAL PULL MOTIVATIONS

Physical pull factors refer to the destination itself, either the exact geographical destination or the physical activities it offers. The geographical pull from a destination is what appeals to the person interested purely in the physical environment, but also includes natural environments that have been altered by mankind to create more attractive areas. Examples include the general topographical qualities of a destination such as mountains, beaches, jungles, and deserts. These are physical geographical pull factors. Tourists looking for pure geographical locations would travel to one beach destination over another, depending on price and proximity. In other words, when a tourist is pulled to a physical location because it is a beach, it is not a particular city, nation, or country for which he or she is looking, just somewhere with the physical attributes toward which he or she is being pulled. Geographical pulls include also specific countries. The tourist may still be pulled toward a country because it has mountains or beaches, but it is different in that the tourist here is attracted to the actual country itself, its culture, and everything it has to offer. Physical motivators to visit a location can also be to see monuments, landmarks, and historical sites. These types of physical attributes can be found in every country. Some tourists are pulled towards the heritage of a specific place, while others are pulled toward any destination, and would enjoy seeking out whatever it is that region has to offer. The Wonders of the World are still some of the most visited places by tourists from all over the world. The actual list of wonders is fluid, changing as the world expands. But often tourists are strongly attracted to these types of sites.

Then there are individuals pulled to a location physically, not because of the natural attributes of the location, but for the physical features and attractions of the destination. This could include the facilities of an accommodation. Often, specific hotels themselves are the destination. The tourist is attracted to a specific type of destination, an all-inclusive resort for example, with little regard to its geographical location. More cities and countries are creating these all-inclusive destinations for tourists due to their popularity. The physical attraction for some of arriving at a location and not having to travel outside of it for anything is appealing. Cruise ships can fall under this umbrella of physical pull motivators. Again, it is a physical location, like those mentioned with all-inclusive destinations. The attraction here, the pull, is to enjoy everything in one location while still physically traveling.

Another type of physical pull to an area is activities. These could include physical activities like skiing, mountain climbing, or surfing as well as attractions like theme parks. The first of the two are activities that the tourist either already enjoys or may want to learn. Sometimes the physical pull towards these activities will affect the geographical location the tourist chooses to travel to, and sometimes, again, it has nothing to do with geography, as long as he or she can enjoy the activity. Theme parks and water parks are almost in a category all by themselves. Similar to the pull of all-inclusive resorts and desirable physical activities, the pull toward organized adventure and activities is for a one-stop vacation where the tourist would not necessarily have to make plans outside of the remote area offering the adventure.

TOURISM INDUSTRY AND PULL MOTIVATORS

The second main pull motivator for a tourist is created by the tourism industry. Again, with the supply and demand example, push and pull factors create very fine lines on who is pushing, who is pulling, when, and why. The tourism industry itself is broken down into so many different parts, with each part playing a different role in the industry as a whole and within the plan of pull motivation. This section will simply explore the pull factors that the tourism industry creates, with a more in-depth view of the working parts behind the scenes of the industry to come later.

The physical pull motivators for a tourist have been described. But where did the tourist get the knowledge about a destination in order to direct their pull-force towards it? When did the destination become *the tourist's* idea? Tourism destinations are constantly working hard to attract potential tourists, instigating a person to come up with what he or she thinks is a personal motive to travel to a particular destination. In other words, there are hundreds and thousands of individual destinations creating information and providing knowledge in direct and indirect ways in order to pull the tourist to them. The word *advertising* comes from the Latin for *turn toward.* The industry uses advertisements to communicate to and persuade tourists to make their locations the tourist's destination. Advertising can be done by nongovernmental organizations like travel agencies and hotel chains, or distributed by governments themselves through tourism ministries or government-owned private sector enterprises. Advertisements produced by governments are able to reach out over land and sea directly to the tourist from any country, in a multitude of ways, as content regulations are minimal.

Advertising to pull in tourists can be broken down into dozens of different types of mediums. Ads can be placed almost anywhere, from billboards and social media to radio, television, and even through celebrities. But the two main types of advertising, in terms of creating a higher tourism pull, are direct and indirect. Direct tourism marketing is generated through paper ads, social media, emails, and through many other media routes. These types of ads for a destination are done with an intent to directly inform a tourist about the destination including details about how to get there, where to stay, and what to do. This type of advertising can have multiple target markets depending on the creators and the distributors of these advertisements. Sometimes places cast out large nets hoping to catch the attention of as many people as possible and reel them in to their destinations. Other times, marketing efforts have a very distinct, direct target market in mind, knowing exactly what type of person would want to come to their locations and targeting them directly. Most destinations in the industry do their homework. They research and analyze as much data as possible about their potential tourists. They are dissecting the tourists' thinking, why and how they are motivated from within, and their desires and needs. The industry and people responsible for "the pull" are studying the tourist and "the push" in order to succeed in their goal of getting tourists.

As a result of their constant researching, they also know how to reach the tourists indirectly. There are a few different general ways to do this. One is through a third party, such as a travel agent or tour company. Nongovernmental and government agencies alike will work with travel agency companies and tour companies. They provide all of the necessary information that the tourist would want to know. When a tourist then contacts one of these companies for help with travel, there are destinations and packages that the company offers which indirectly puts that destination into the mind of the tourist. Another method of indirect advertising is through print ads or the Internet. Placing ads in places over which people often glance, knowingly or not, is a huge piece of reaching the tourist. Billboards that people often walk by or drive by, popular magazines that a person flips through, and the Internet advertisements that are hidden as well as pop up annoyingly are constantly being viewed by our minds' eyes whether or not we realize it. This is indirect marketing. Imagine one day waking up after contemplating where to go on vacation and suddenly sure that *you* finally decided where you wanted to go, not realizing that that exact destination has been advertised on the billboard you drive by every day, on the website you frequent for research, and in a magazine on your coffee table. Not once did you read the ads, but now you suddenly want to go the place in them. Marketing objective: complete.

CONSUMERISM

The marketing efforts of the tourism industry flow directly into the topic of consumerism and how they have been entwined as a pull factor for tourists. First, I want to look at the word's history and the journey to its modern meaning. *Consumerism* simply means the acquisition of goods and services in massive quantities. But originally, *consumerism* meant that the consumer should be an informed decision maker, therefore able to gather and be given information from the market. This led to the concept that the marketplace should be responsible for ensuring fair economic practices, which led to the creation of policies and laws that manufacturers had to follow in order to sell safely. This progressed to a definition of studying, regulating, or interacting with the marketplace. At the same time this definition of *consumerism* was developing, another quite different explanation of the word started forming. This defined *consumerism* as meaning high levels of consumption. It then turned into the act of selfishly collecting products or economic materials, before evolving into the definition of a force from the marketplace that destroys individuality, harms society, and influenced by globalization.

Today, consumerism is a pull factor for the tourist. The need, created by time, society, the marketplace, and globalization, to acquire things, has grown to include the need to acquire travel. It is another force that has assisted in the indirect programming of the tourist's mind, drawing him or her toward travel, vacations, and holidays, and engrained it as if it is actually a primal need. But today, consumerism and travel are modern primal needs in life. People have slowly started to enjoy having more tangible things rather than intangible, and holidays have become part of that. Just as the tourist has evolved through time, so have marketing plans and so have the personal needs of humankind. This is not to say that all people fit this harsh definition of always needing "more," but tourists have been affected, some directly and some indirectly, by the idea, which has created a pull motivation. And as we have explored both the push and pull of the tourist, you can see that it is not always a black and white situation when discussing why the tourist went to a destination. It's a combination, a back and forth, of push and pull that gets the tourist from one place to another.

TOURIST EXPLORATIONS

To understand what it is the tourist wants to do during his or her travels and explorations, there has to be some basic separation of the types of tourists. Yes, they all fall under an internal motivation which is what got them moving in the first place, and, yes, most were also affected by external pulls to destinations. But what one does when at the destination of one's "choice" depends on the type of person. Explorations can include everything from the most extreme physical activities to choosing which beach to spend the day reading under an umbrella. Although very different from each other, explorations are relative. Just as people are different in their everyday lives, many different things motivate tourists.

TYPES OF TOURISTS ON THE SPECTRUM

Not everybody wants to zip-line through the jungle nor does every traveler enjoy being enclosed in an all-inclusive environment cut off from the local culture. There is a spectrum of travelers. One end of the spectrum is the pure adventurist.

This tourist seeks out the most exotic locations with the highest level of adventure activities, preferably of an unknown variety. On the other end of the spectrum, you will find the tourist who simply needs a break from it all. This tourist is often most comfortable in locations that remind him or her of home in terms of the day-to-day surroundings, and just wants to relax outside of his or her current life. The best thing about a spectrum is that a tourist doesn't have to stay on one part of it, nor does that part define him or her. Rather, during different eras of one's life, one may start out at an end of the spectrum, yet later in life enjoy traveling on another part of it. The spectrum can be broken down into five sections for ease of description: the adventurer, the loner, the culturist, the independent, and the organized tourist.

THE ADVENTURER AND THE LONER

The adventurer and the loner are very close on the spectrum because they both have their own personal motivations and agendas for travel that rarely involve making plans with others. The difference is in the terms themselves. The adventurers seek out adventurous explorations. They plan their travels to places with exotic landscapes full of dangerous, risk-taking activities. Whether they plan out their activities ahead of time or not, these tourists will be traveling solely to explore physically challenging activities. The loners, on the other hand, although they prefer to plan their trips alone as well, are looking to blend right in to the local communities. They prefer to travel alone, and when they arrive in a foreign country, they immediately seek out explorations that will immerse them into the communities at hand. These tourists will rarely reach out to or involve themselves with any other tourists or organized tourist activities.

THE EXPLORER

These tourists are the true explorers. They balance on the spectrum in that they do not want to solely disappear into the local community nor seek adventures on their own for the sake of a rush, but they do want to be part of the local community and take part in explorations within it. They often do not tap into the tourism industry for direct assistance in planning travel and accommodations nor do they take part in local tourism industry setups, such as inclusive hotels or restaurants run by the local industry. These tourists are eager to explore and experience the social and cultural lifestyle of their chosen destinations. They will eat at local eateries, and if possible, within the local residences' presence. Their explorations are motivated by culture.

THE INDEPENDENT AND ORGANIZED

Although these two tourists are near the same end of the spectrum, there are still big differences that set them apart. The independent tourists may use organized resources from the tourism industry such as a travel website or travel agency. They might also still partake in daily tours during part of their travels. But these tourists, while enjoying the organization of travel planning, will take off on their own to explore their destinations unassisted. They tend to have the best of both worlds in travel, utilizing all of their options, but not strictly adhering to one particular type of trip or another. The organized tourist rounds out the far end of the spectrum. Unlink the independent tourist, this tourist prefers a highly organized holiday with little to no contact with the destination's culture or host community. This type of holiday is often entwined with all-inclusive packages where the tourists partake in no exploration on their own. Instead, their destinations are bubbles, offering them just what they need, which is usually just an escape from their daily surroundings.

ACTIVITIES AND ATTRACTIONS

When any tourist is considering travel, he or she has to consider not only a destination, prompted by a myriad of internal and external forces, but must decide also exactly *what* he or she wants to do during his or her travels. The *what* can be just as important as the *where*, more so for some travelers than others. But overall, every tourist, no matter where he or she is on the spectrum, is faced with choosing activities while at his or her destination. Some tourists first pick a location and then find activities in the region they would like to explore. Or they decide what activities they want to partake in or discover, and then pick the location based on what the different destinations offer. For example, the organized tourist may know exactly what he or she wants in an all-inclusive package. But when he or she arrives, he or she will have to make choices still on what restaurant in the resort at which to eat or by which pool to spend the days. Although these are not the same type of choices in exploration the adventurer would have to face, they are still choices in exploration relative to the tourist and the destination.

The activities people have been doing on holidays has changed over time as dramatically as the motivations to travel. In our recent history, people traditionally traveled over a weekend, craving locations such as the beach, concentrating on relaxing for the weekend. Travel trends now exist on a spectrum of one- or two-night short breaks to taking off six months to a year as a "break." The general content itself during a holiday has changed as well. For example, those with children would often find a comfortable accommodation where their children could safely play while they relax. In contrast, a family today could pack up and take the whole family halfway around the world for a cultural experience. Activity-filled and adventure-filled holidays have become more of the norm for the tourist family.

The three elements to traveling are the region of origin, the transit, and the destination. The region of origin is where the tourist begins. All of the motivations to travel swirl around the tourist in this spot, decisions are made, and this is the place from which the tourist will push off toward the chosen destination. Part of making plans at this stage include not only choosing a destination and booking accommodations, but also choosing the method in which one will travel: the transit. Plane, train, boat, bicycle, automobile, or foot are all part of the journey itself. So are the activities that the tourist takes part in at the destination.

For some, planning out all of these activities is part of planning for the trip. Some activities can be booked directly ahead of time. Frequently, travelers who enjoy being prepared will book a tour or two in advance of arriving. Paper maps are still in use, in comparison with only electronic ones, for many tourists. They give them a general sense of direction, and they are able to map out their stops and activities ahead of time on them. If the tourist planned his or her holiday specifically because of a pull to a specific location that has activities he or she enjoys, he or she is all the better prepared and aware of what to expect. There is an opposite of this busy, organized traveler and that is the explorer. One's surroundings can be explored without heavy planning ahead of time, and this type of tourist prefers to stay busy by beginning explorations when he or she arrives at the destination, not before. Both types of tourists often enjoy the same activities. The only difference is that some already know what those are and some can't wait to find out!

But what exactly is the modern tourist *doing* on holiday? This simply goes hand in hand with what motivated the tourist to go to this particular destination to begin with. For example, those on leisure holiday prefer leisure activities like swimming, sunbathing, or reading. The tourist seeking an adventure will most likely seek out destinations that can curb that appetite by offering active sports-like activities such as zip-lining, mountain climbing, or water-skiing. And for the cultural enthusiast, guided tours around an historical region with in-depth exposure to the local population would suffice.

And all tourists, pushed from and pulled by every motivation, will partake in eating. Searching for and exploring local cuisine is an activity taken up by all tourists. The degree to which this becomes more or less of an activity depends on the traveler. The tourist focused on food tourism will make the process of eating most like an activity. Having traveled to his or her location for the sole purpose of cultural cuisine exploration, every meal is a celebration. The other extreme tourist in terms of food tourism is the tourist who only eats to live and does not live to eat. These tourists often find that eating in their hotels or near their accommodations is the easiest solution to the problem, and receive the least enjoyment from the activity.

EXPECTATIONS AND SATISFACTION

We all have expectations for everything, whether we realize it or not. And so does the tourist. With expectations come levels of satisfaction and dissatisfaction. An expectation is a strong belief that something will happen or be the case in the future. Tourists expect the best of the future when it pertains to travels they have planned. But sometimes it can happen the opposite way. A tourist can have low expectations of an accommodation he or she has booked at a low price but be amazed upon arrival, increasing his or her level of satisfaction.

Later chapters will discuss how the vendor or business sets up expectations *for* the guest and the detailed planning that goes into that. This section, however, is looking out from the tourists' eyes and minds to see what they expect from their transit and destination and their travel plans on a whole. Keep in mind that expectations and satisfaction levels can change at any moment! For example, if you are at a fine dining destination enjoying your meal and a waiter walks by your table, trips, and begins to mutter profanities as he picks up the dropped items from his tray, the level of satisfaction from what you expected will drop immediately and dramatically. You cannot forget the incident as the evening goes on, nor can you expect the same level of enjoyment from the atmosphere from when you entered.

Businesses work hard to set up an environment that will exceed the expectations of guests. This being written, not all businesses work equally hard. Does that mean we expect less from an inexpensive dining venue than from an expensive one? It does, sometimes. Society has programmed the tourist and the guest to expect less from less expensive goods or services. Are you not worried when you find an item online for $200 less than its average price as to whether the item is going to meet the same expectations as the original would? The same goes for the tourist and his or her travels. But it has become commonplace to book travel in packages, creating a much lower price when one purchases transit and accommodations together. Does this mean those same airlines or hotels are going to be below your expectations because you got a good deal? Not necessarily. Goods, and even services, over time have become consumerized. This being written, how else is the tourist to expect one place to be better than another, if not the price? Experience.

Businesses have to focus now not only on the goods and services they provide, but on the experiences they provide. Unfortunately, this spot-on idea to increase levels of satisfaction and exceed the guests' expectations, creating more revenue, has not caught on at all of the businesses or sectors in the tourism industry. Take the airline industry. How often do travelers rave about one particular airline experience over another, putting small incidences aside? A majority of people that book a flight for a holiday merely compare airline ticket costs because there is no overpowering experience one provides over another. The goods are still comparable, such as the cost to check luggage or the amenities of food and movies. But there are no jaw-dropping experiences that create a buzz in the airline industry. That is not to say that expectations from a traveler aboard an airline cannot still be exceeded by excellent customer service. But has anybody ever described a flight where it felt like he or she was transported to another realm and forgot he or she was on a flight the whole time? If so, please let me know!

But let's back up and take a look at how expectations start and where they go as the tourist moves through his or her travels. When most people plan a trip, they hope for the best. But expectations can change before the trip even begins.

Flights can be delayed within a second's notice or rental car locations may not have the car expected at pickup. As soon as the expectation changes, the level of satisfaction does as well. Even though a flight to another country is extremely pleasant with customer service that exceeds expectations, if that flight lands and gets stuck on the tarmac for two hours after landing with the air conditioner not working and the demand you stay in your seat, the experience has changed. Although 99% of the experience on the plane ride was high in satisfaction, the last part of the journey made you forget completely about that. If asked what your review of the airline and flight would be, most likely you would say horrible, without even mentioning how the majority of the flight exceeded your expectations.

Realistically, anything can happen at any time during a tourist's trip that would change his or her satisfaction level. This is not pessimistic, but realistic.

The next part of the journey after transit is the arrival at the destination. This could be at an airport, or by car, or boat. Again, most travelers expect for things to go smoothly, that their arrival at their destinations will be flawless, and that they will easily make their way to their booked accommodations with ease. That's not to imply that things will go awry. Lost luggage or transportation from an airport to a hotel being unavailable for hours can put a dark cloud over the tourist's mind, and drop expectations right away from a smooth and optimistic to pessimistic and terrible. But the tourist is on a journey filled with variables, so it's best to go with the flow and expect change.

Accommodations are major players in journeys when it comes to expectations. This leads back to the experiences. Often tourists make plans for accommodations based on their affordability. Sometimes hotels are booked at such a low rate, the tourist is realistic in low expectations. And often those expectations are met. It is when the expectations are exceeded that the satisfaction level soars. What could make satisfaction levels hit an all-time high is the experience created by the accommodation or destination. For example, have you ever stayed in a hotel where every single staff member smiled at you as you passed by, or greeted you and offered assistance?Did this increase your overall satisfaction of the stay? If so, then you have experienced that for which the smartest businesses in the industry have strived. These businesses have found out how to create a total experience, utilizing every tool in the toolbox to exceed offering merely excellent goods and services.

Lodging consists of a number of puzzle pieces that if not linked together correctly can constantly affect the guest's level of satisfaction. If these pieces are not on cue with the whole experience as mentioned above, guests can find themselves constantly feeling the ups and downs of the destination as if the business's problems are now their own. Such pieces include the room itself, and its size, cleanliness, and location on the property. The onsite restaurants and bars under the hotel's umbrella can also present challenges to the guests' expectations.

There are endless variables to a transit operation or accommodation at one's destination that can alter a tourist's satisfaction level within seconds. There is no way to consistently stay at the same level of satisfaction through an entire trip. But there are ways to experience a consistent level of satisfaction, higher than one's expectations, when one finds that hotel, restaurant, resort, or even community that creates that all-encompassing experience: an experience that pushes all of the sensory buttons of the guest, an experience that is flawless in its delivery of goods and services every time. This is a place that a tourist leaves, and returns home only to find that place left an impression on them that he or she is happy to and eager to call upon as often as possible. The question is why don't all businesses take advantage of this way of presenting themselves as a whole experience? What is holding them back from stepping up their presentation? These questions cannot be answered by the tourist, but only by the business of tourism itself.

Part Three
The Business of Tourism

The travel and tourism industry is made up of several moving parts that, when moving in unison, thrust the industry forward into infinite possibilities. But there are two integral, opposite, and magnetic pieces that are essential in keeping the sector moving: the tourist and the industry. As previously discussed, there would be no tourism industry without the tourist and there is no question as to what came first. The tourism industry does have a long history, in fact, but it does not go back to the beginning of mankind like the tourist. Out of a need to serve and cater to the tourist, the sector eventually flourished and became a vital part to the economic survival of many countries. But before the 1950s, the moving parts of the sector were not working together as a team. Hotels, transit companies, and travel agencies all worked independently. International travel was still only for the privileged. But eventually, the two began taking steps towards combined efforts after 1950. As hotel operators received more demands from guests, they began to create amenities in their establishments. It was truly the emergence of business centers in hotels as well as shops and arcades. People began to have more leisure time, with an increase in employers offering paid time off from work. Air transit took off also, which helped mold the tourism industry. By the 1980s and 1990s, air transport had improved and private businesses were aiding in the details of holidays, from transit to accommodations. Although the travel and tourism sector was still not considered a global industry worth organizing, there was still a large enough group that did recognize the potential and importance of the sector with optimism. These people became the leaders who started forming an organized industry that is now one of the top economic sectors in the world.

ECONOMIC SECTORS

To get an idea of where the tourism industry sits in the bigger picture, it is necessary to examine economic sectors. A sector is an area of the economy in which businesses share the same or related products or services. Most nations have their own economic categories, but globally, the economy is broken down into five separate sectors. The dividing of the economy is useful for many reasons and for many players in the global economic game. The division allows for further in-depth analysis of the economy as a whole. The way the economy is divided is seen as a continuum of distance from the natural environment.

The first tier, or primary sector, concerns itself with the utilization of raw materials and the extraction and harvesting of these natural products from the Earth through agriculture, farming, fishing, hunting, mining, and forestry. Also part of this primary sector is the processing and packaging of the raw materials. It is no surprise that the percentage of workers in this category has decreased dramatically over the past one hundred years. In some countries, only a single-digit percentage of the population's workforce falls into this primary sector. From the first sector comes the secondary sector, which is responsible for manufacturing finished goods including the processing, manufacturing, and construction of final products. This sector involves metalworking, automobile production, textile production, chemical and engineering industries, aerospace manufacturing, energy utilities, engineering, brewers and bottlers, construction, and ship building. This second tier made up the largest population of the workforce in many countries during the twenty-first century. Factory workers made up the big boom in the manufacturing business, but is fading out as other sectors further distanced from natural resources grow in size globally.

The third tier is the tertiary sector that provides services to businesses and the general population. This sector includes retail sales, entertainment, transportation, restaurants, media, insurance, healthcare, financial services, and also encompasses the tourism industry. The tertiary sector currently holds the largest portion of the workforce in most developed as well as developing countries around the world. The next tier, the quaternary sector, is responsible for innovative services, which includes intellectual pursuits like education as well as government, cultural, libraries, scientific research, and information technology. The last tier is called the quinary sector and has stemmed most closely from the quaternary sector. This section includes the highest levels of decision making in a society or economy. It contains the top executives or officials in government, science, universities, nonprofit, healthcare, cultural, and media enterprises. It is also known as the human services. Some nations recognize domestic activities such as stay-at-home-parents or homemakers in this category, even though they do not yield a financial gain, but are still recognized as important activities that contribute to the society.

The tertiary sector of the economy is referred to as the service sector, or the service industry. This is where the tourism industry sits. This sector provides affective labor, which is defined as work carried out intended to produce or modify emotional experiences in people, also referred to as invisible labor. This definition alone is what drives the tourism industry and every business involved in it. This sector in the economy has a heavy focus on the production of services in contrast to the production and distribution of goods. Even though it is the provider of intangible goods, it runs as any other business in the economy. With business plans, goals, research, analysis, consumers, and products, the service industry is one of the most up-and-coming competitive markets on a global scale. With tourism numbers soaring worldwide, this sector has actually surpassed other sectors of the world economy such as the raw materials and manufacturing sectors. Today, the service industry accounts for more than three fifths of the world gross domestic product (GDP), employing over one third of the worldwide labor force.

There is a simple explanation for how the world shifted from the primary sector of sourcing natural resources to the service industry being the leading sector in the economy. The production of goods, from gathering to processing, has become mechanized, and each year more efficiently so. Because this use of machines requires less human labor to produce tangible goods, the service functions of management, distribution, finance, and sales have become relatively more important to the process. Another source driving the increase of the services industry is businesses that are beginning to realize the functionality of outsourcing different parts of their business structure. Not only are they outsourcing activities that are directly part of their businesses, but companies are also recognizing how professional services such as consultancy, training, and marketing can directly help them improve their performances as businesses. This creates a win-win situation for the individuals and small businesses providing these services and the larger companies utilizing them. And in general, individuals are also becoming more service oriented and less materials oriented; with less focus on material needs, consumers are highly in tune with the quality of services they demand.

GLOBAL TOURISM ORGANIZATIONS

There are a few global organizations that have set themselves up over the past few decades to help promote the travel and tourism sector for countries aiming to drive economic growth and environmental sustainability, and to lend support and knowledge about tourism policies worldwide. The UNWTO (United Nations World Tourism Organization) is the most recognizable of these officialdoms. In the late 1940s, after the Second World War, the International Union of Official Travel Organizations (IUOTO) restructured to promote tourism in response to the increasing numbers of international travelers. They were presented as an international trade component and offered economic development strategies for developing nations. But by the late 1960s, the IUOTO needed further transformation to enhance its role on an international level. In 1967, their general assembly decided that they needed to further the organization's goals by making an intergovernmental body that had the ability to function on an international level in cooperation with other international agencies, especially the United Nations. This resulted in the forming of the World Tourism Organization (WTO) in 1970, which officially launched in 1974. It was not until 2003 that the general council agreed to make the WTO a specialized agency of the United Nations in order to increase the visibility of the WTO, which then became the UNWTO. As of 2014, the membership of the UNWTO was at 156 countries and had over 400 affiliate members that represent tourism associations, educational institutions, the private sector, and local tourism authorities. They hold themselves responsible for being a global forum for tourism policy issues as they promote responsible, sustainable, and universally accessible tourism, with a focus on developing countries.

Another global group is the World Travel and Tourism Council (WTTC), the leading private sector international tourism organization. It was established in 1990 out of the need for more data relating to the travel and tourism industry; at that time, it was not highly recognized as an essential industry for economic strength. They currently provide research in conjunction with the economic and social impact of the travel and tourism industry. They also organize a Global Summit every year in April and oversee the Tourism for Tomorrow Awards in many categories to acknowledge and encourage developments in sustainable tourism. The WTTC is also responsible for forming the Tourism Satellite Account (TSA) in 1999 in order to compile and publish data. It is now the main tool for economic measurement in tourism. They strive to standardize the methodical framework for tourism statistics and are also responsible for reinforcing international comparability of tourism statistical data, helping nations develop their own system of tourism statistics, and fostering the macroeconomic analysis of tourism. In other words, they are the accumulators, analyzers, and promoters of tourism data for all to use.

IMPACT OF TOURISM ON THE WORLD ECONOMY

The travel and tourism industry is an important, and for some countries, vital, source of income. The significance tourism has on a country reaches far beyond the businesses involved. The sector is essential to the life of a nation, with its power directly hitting not only the economic balance, but also the cultural, educational, and social sectors as well as touching its international relations. Tourism has its grasp on every part of a nation, and although the effect can be widely positive and game changing for some countries, for others, it is a bit more challenging to see the positive effect through negative circumstances. In terms of the industry's economic contribution to the world GDP and employment, it has been increasingly successful for years past, with no signs of letting up.

The WTTC releases an annual report that summarizes the economic impact of travel and tourism as well as offers forecasts for the year ahead. It provides hard evidence to aid public and private businesses with their own policy making and investment decisions having to do with travel and tourism. With detailed information about how the industry directly hits the world GDP, public and private bodies alike are able to confidently make the best decisions.The GDP is a comprehensive measure of production that is equivalent to the sum of the gross values of all resident and institutional units engaged in production, accounting for any taxes minus subsidies, on products not already included in the value of their output. The GDP is used to measure both a particular industry's contribution and the contribution of a nation or country as a whole. It measures value, not sales, which compares one nation to another. In other words, it is a profit-and-loss statement on a global scale, taking a value and subtracting the value of goods that are used up in producing it. What many people look to the GDP for is the general growth of an economy from year to year. It is used as a guide to determine success or failure of economic policy, and can further decide if an economy is in recession.

Travel and tourism is one of the biggest players on the global economic growth front. According to the 2015 annual update and summary report of the economic impact of trade and tourism, its direct contribution to the GDP was US$2.4 trillion in 2014, which equaled 9.8% of the entire global economy. The sector created over two million new direct jobs in the sector, impacting global employment by a 2.3% increase. Travel and tourism outperformed leading sectors in growth on a global level, including automotive, financial services, aerospace, public services, retail, and extraction. The industry also outperformed the wider economies of countries such as Greece and Sri Lanka. As predicted, the industry maintained a strong, positive growth for the fifth year in a row and proved to perform as a key factor in continued global growth and job creation. The sector and the overall world GDP was below forecast slightly, attesting to unexpected world developments that could lower expected growth. Year after year, global incidents, political instability, terror attacks, oil prices, and mass illness can all add to or subtract from the overall rate of economic growth for a country or the world.

IMPACT OF TOURISM ON THE NATION

Just like the travel and tourism industry helps shape the world economy, each and every individual nation is affected uniquely by it. Like any business, tourism needs to be managed effectively with not only the bottom line in mind but the livelihood of the people driving it. When the scale tips and the financial benefits become more important than the industry's sustainability to a nation, negativity ripples through the region, causing distress to the host community and the environment. Most nations have managers of their tourism sector called

Destination Marking Organizations (DMO), often referred to as tourism authorities, among other groups like a convention and visitor or travel bureau. These organizations are focused on drawing tourists to their regions, and are responsible for creating the tourism strategy for their nation. They are there to promote the sustainable development of the tourism industry, and support activities in the industry responsibly in order to create growth for their economy while protecting the community. These authorities often oversee regulations within sector businesses, licensing, and supervision of businesses involved as well as activities related to the tourism industry of their areas. They also offer assistance by conducting research, and providing factual data and information to keep the nations maximizing the potential of the travel and tourism industry. The authority may also be in charge of the cleanliness and aesthetic factors of the areas in their regions most visited by tourists. They are the nation's tourism managers.

Tourism has many positive direct impacts on a nation. Employment is one of the biggest positive additions to a local tourist area; tourism creates jobs for the host community both directly for the tourism industry and indirectly in businesses such as local retailers or transportation companies. Organizations in charge of tourism for their nation can truly give back to a local community by being aware of eco-tourism, which includes the host community providing sustainable jobs to the local people, which in turn improves the nation's economic situation while decreasing poverty. Particularly in developing countries, but still important to all, hiring local residents from the host community provides jobs to some who may not have been able to find work, and it opens up the development of skills for the local people for employment opportunities at that time and in the future. Local communities anywhere in the world know more about their local habitat and culture than anybody else. Their expertise in their own cities, nations, or cultures makes them the best people for the job.

Indirect employment in the tourism industry helps generate some of the same positive results within the community. Indirect jobs include those with local businesses, often in retail, hospitality, transportation, or attractions. These jobs also provide stability for the industry, and with consistent tourist traffic, the jobs are stable and consistent. As long as tourism continues to thrive, the job market for local people across the world remains stable as well. Small businesses are one of the biggest pieces of the tourism industry. They make up every destination's environment with their goods and services. A tourist may be drawn to a specific destination for a certain reason. But it is not until he or she gets there that he or she begins to experience the location that is very strongly molded by the host community and the local businesses. The choices they make for their businesses, including whom they employ, all feed into the bigger picture of the nation's image. Tourism's effect on local businesses is huge. It provides them with the opportunity to thrive beyond the business brought in by the locals.Especially in rural areas, small businesses are directly affected when they are given the opportunity to work in conjunction with the tourism industry by being supported and also promoted by the tourism authority, funneling business directly to them.

Socially, a community has the opportunity to preserve its culture and traditional jobs, which play a big part in tourism. For example, the tourism industry often encourages regional customs and festivals that might have died out over the years. These activities draw in the cultural tourist as well as gain interest and revenue from all tourists visiting the area.

Souvenirs are also a huge sector of the tourism industry within a nation, again, encouraging the host community to continue creating handicrafts that reflect its culture and can be sold to tourists. The interactions that tourists have with the host community and the cultural understanding they gain not only create interest and curiosity from the visitors, but it can boost awareness of the challenges the nation faces, which often raises global awareness.

Tourism can not only help preserve the culture of a nation, but it again raises awareness and can preserve the wildlife and natural resources as well provide many environmental advantages. Resources such as bodies of water that are being over-fished or polluted, or rainforests that may be facing deforestation, can become assets to the tourism industry. With this attention, more awareness and physical action is brought on by the local authorities to give more attention to preserving these areas out of concern not only for the region, but out of concern of the economic growth directly related to tourism. Sometimes it takes an outside view or opinion to generate inner action.

There are two sides to any subject matter. The impact of tourism on a nation can be positive, but it can also carry negative effects if the sector is not well managed overall. The negative aspects can be the same as the positive ones mentioned above. The strength of the infrastructure holds the foundation together for the tourism industry. In most nations, there are funds set aside that go right back into the economy, and this is what is used to fix and maintain roads, tourism industry businesses, and visitor centers. So if the government is not putting the money from the industry back into the nation, the infrastructure starts to crumble. Although heavy tourist flow can bring jobs and employment to an area for the local community, it can also take them away. Jobs in the industry that can be abundant in one nation can be destructive in another. Some nations have tourist seasons due to weather. When traveling is seasonal, so are the jobs. This leaves the local community unemployed during the off season, making their jobs temporary and seasonal which means there are no full-time benefits from the positions, either. Seasonal jobs can also mean poorly paid positions. Some regions do not even have a hand in hiring their own community for tourism positions. When huge, international hotels and businesses plant themselves in tourist destinations, they also bring along foreign staff to work for their companies instead of hiring the local community.

Unfortunately, not all of the money generated by the tourism industry goes back into the destination. Oftentimes, that money gets funneled back out to international hotel chains or transportation companies, instead of staying with local businesses or people. Small businesses are heavily affected by the tourism industry, and when it is a negative influence, small businesses that would normally flourish from an increase in visitors can actually fail. Again, when bigger, international businesses move in that offer the same goods or services in an all-inclusive environment, the local small businesses not only lose out on customers, but are put out of business sometimes by these bigger businesses.

Another negative effect of tourism on a nation, not necessarily having to do with the management or infrastructure, is social, brought on by tourist behavior. Not all tourists have caught on to the ecotourism movement that guides tourists to be kind visitors to their destinations. Masses of tourists can bring negativity to the quality of life of a community. Tourists can bring in or encourage drug and alcohol problems, add to the congestion and crowding of an area, and bring inflated levels of crime. Local cultures and values can be crushed by masses of tourists instead of flourish. Environmentally, the attraction of more and more tourists can lead to the destruction of a region's natural and cultural resources through overuse or misuse. Air pollution, littering, and sewage problems are brought on also by the visit of the masses to a singular destination.

It is unfortunate, but most of these negative effects are happening to developing countries and those with just poor infrastructure. When they already have a weak link in their systems, they can be easily affected by these things as well as terrorism, natural disasters, political instability, and economic recessions. But whether or not a nation is ready for masses of travelers, it can be negatively influenced by tourism. The only way to counter this and to attempt to make the industry a positive experience for the region is to be prepared. Again, the industry is a business and every business must have a plan, a mission, a vision, and a strategy to reach its tourism goals and objectives. In order to ensure long-term sustainability, a nation must use these as a guide as well as adopt a continuous improvement policy.

But is there a formula for a nation to yield solid economic growth from tourism? There are definitely internal components of a nation that make for a naturally successful tourist destination and business. Some of the variables within a destination that can impact its success are the local economy, the natural environment, and its infrastructure. But does that mean they are automatically going to succeed if they have all of these things in line? Or the opposite: Will they be destined to fail if they cannot manage all of them successfully? Neither is the answer. For example, say a local economy has lower local prices and excellent exchange rates that would attract money-conscious tourists who would then in turn automatically influence how well the region is doing economically, which has a direct effect on the infrastructure. Higher local prices could possibly do the opposite, and discourage tourists from coming to the area, which would negatively affect the local businesses and tourism industry, directly adding to a poor national infrastructure. But surprisingly enough, money doesn't always matter in this particular situation. In fact, most tourists do not look at the exchange rate or the local prices of goods when determining their holiday destinations. As we learned earlier, tourists have many more emotion-driven motivations that push them towards destinations. Also, in terms of pull factors, cities and nations do not typically advertise their local economic statuses in their marketing plans.

What really makes for a successful tourist destination is a balanced approach to the destination's management, which includes a business plan and a tourism strategy with many different kinds of data. The tourism industry in a nation is complex with many possible influences, and should be treated as any business would be. The managers of a nation's tourism sector should be constantly supervising all of the factors of the local industries, reviewing data and information about the global industry, analyzing and providing support based off of the information collected, and constantly changing based on this information. The most successful businesses anywhere in the world have been flawless at balancing the successful constants of a business with the factors that require constant change in tune with customer, in this case, the tourist, demands. In order to secure long-term sustainability, a nation must be able to strategize what it is their region has naturally and what systems already work well in their tourism business to help determine their next steps to get them to their goals. This planning and ongoing management of the sector will contribute to continuing improvements and success.

KEY PLAYERS: MARKETING AND BRANDING

The travel and tourism industry is stacked with invaluable key players. These are individuals and groups working at every level as a team to make their destination the tourist's destination. With guiding organizations like the WTCC and UNWTO, cities and nations are able to tap into valuable information to help internally organize their tourism business structures to successfully utilize their local communities while presenting their brands globally. There are five major parts to the travel and tourism industry: travel websites and agencies, rental car agencies, hotel and air companies, local businesses, the host community, and the location's tourism authority. All of these components are connected with one goal in mind: to attract business to a specific region. And one element of doing so keeps those gears turning in particular: destination marketing. In order for a location to keep its hand in the global cookie jar, it must pull tourists to visit its destination. As established previously, the "push" and "pull" of the industry are delicately interwoven, with the tourist providing the "push" towards a destination, the personal motivation, and the industry creating the "pull." The strength behind that pull is marketing and branding.

Mentioned earlier as one of the pull motivators of the tourism industry, marketing is used to reach a target audience and persuade it to take action towards obtaining something, usually goods or services. In the tourism industry, every position takes part in a marketing campaign, from the host community and the small businesses of a destination to the large accommodation and transit companies all the way up to the nation itself. There are so many different modes of advertising that it is no surprise to find that we are the target of marketing efforts all the time, from the tourism industry and every other business today. As mentioned in chapter two, there are both direct and indirect advertising techniques. This simply means sometimes we are aware we are viewing an ad and sometimes we are not. The best type of marketing reaches a person when he or she least expects it. We are repeatedly led to believe that ads were made for us specifically and are convinced we were just thinking about the need or want for that good or service. This means the promoter of the advertisement has done his or her job well! But what came first: the ad or our inkling of the idea?

Some destinations spend more time on the pulling in of tourists than others. There are locations that have more of a natural gravitation to them, can take part in marketing on a global level, and attract as many tourists as they want with ease. Other locations, however, need to be a little more convincing, or even just provide explanations of what they offer, to pull the tourist to their destinations. This is where cities and nations get into branding. Branding aims at building up a city's or nation's image and reputation to produce an impression, a magnetic pull, for the tourist to the destination. The businesses inside the destination are also doing their part to bring in tourists by producing advertisements tailored to the tourist and promoting their hotels, restaurants, or activities before the tourist's arrival and during the booking stages. Then once the tourist is at the location, the region is still hard at work pulling and tugging at the tourist constantly to use its services or buy its goods. It's a team effort all around to reach the tourist and attract his or her attention. Branding is not an idea unique to tourism. Rather, it is one of the foundational building blocks of every single business in the world. Some have to work harder than others at establishing one, some have their brands naturally built by word of mouth and nurtured, and many other businesses have to work hard through marketing and ads to hammer their brand into consumers' minds.

TRAVEL WEBSITES AND AGENCIES

The origin to every tourist's adventure is the spark of motivation. Next comes the planning stage. Sometimes a tourist has internally established his or her motivation to travel, and has picked a destination based on that; oftentimes, the tourist has done some research into the location and thought of a specific time to visit. In this case, he or she is all ready to make travel plans. On the other hand, there are those tourists who have general internal motivations to travel, but are unable to pinpoint exactly where it is they want to go, what they want to do, and even when they want to go. These travelers often reach out to travel websites and agencies in the planning first, instead of last. Either way, the tourist's travel plans usually end up in the hands of others, whether physically or electronically. And the easiest way to do so is through a travel agency or travel website.

These websites and agencies are where the tourist is going to find the best deals for his or her travel plans. When an agency or website is used by you, it is able to book your travel with transportation, accommodation, and even activities through one booking. The ease of using these venues for travel planning has made them the most commonly used way of booking travel. Package deals, or even just booking through a website with endless offers, is cheaper for the tourist and more convenient.

But what the tourist doesn't know is that he or she is not always the one steering the decisions in these travel plans. There is often an underlying ulterior motive behind the scenes that is pulling, pulling, pulling at the strings.

One might think that travel websites and agencies were merely there to help take one where one wants to go, which they are. But that's not all. What most people don't know is that these travel websites and agencies are advertising machines! What the tourist cannot see is the business relationship that these websites and agencies have with destinations all over the world. They are the suppliers for the airlines, rental car companies, hotel chains, cruise lines, and package tour companies. Although the agent's or website's main task is to help plan travel, sometimes they are weighted more heavily with an opinion that is based on destinations with which they have a business relationship. Their agendas and motivations may not be what their mission statements suggest; rather, they have separate agendas to follow. Although they are not stocked up on travel tickets as a store is with goods, they do have the ability to get those tickets at a discounted rate from all of the destinations in their book of contacts, and oftentimes, have promised to sell a certain number of those tickets to travelers every quarter. In other words, agencies and websites are making a commission between the price the tourist pays for a ticket and the price they pay to the supplier.

Every destination handles these types of transactions differently. Some airline companies do not even offer discounted tickets to agencies in some countries. Other companies pay agencies and website companies a set fee every month, just for advertising their destinations. Whatever role an agency or website plays in the tourist's planning stage, they are an advertisement representative for the destination. Cities and nations have no better direct access to their target audience than they do through these agencies and websites. With their setup, they have the undivided attention from the tourist at a crucial stage in his or her planning. Again, even those searching the Internet in pursuit of a destination idea are going to come across a travel website, or 100 travel websites, driven just by their curiosity. But this is how destinations start to tug at the tourist. If a tourist didn't know where he or she wanted to go before getting on the Internet to do research, he or she may be even more conflicted because of overwhelming ideas afterwards or convinced that the chosen destination is where he or she always inwardly wanted to go in the first place. It can be almost exhausting with one advertisement linking to another and so on. But from the side of the industry, this is exactly what they wanted when they designed and created these advertisements, and made the connections they did with the agencies and websites as their portal.

HOTEL, AIRLINE, AND RENTAL CAR COMPANIES

Tourists can opt out of using travel agencies and websites when planning their travels as well. There are a few reasons for this. For example, this is the way most people used to book travel. Before there was accessibility to travel websites, most people booked the parts of their travel separately. This means they contacted airlines directly to book their flights, and the hotels directly to book their accommodations, as well as any other activities they were interested in exploring on their holidays. Because this is the way it was done before, that's still the way some people book their travel. In other words, sometimes technology changes and people do not change with it. Another scenario is a tourist who is only looking to book one part of his or her journey; for example, an airline trip. In this case, he or she can directly, via the Internet or phone, book his or her flight. All websites for airlines, rental cars, and most hotels still have deals on their homepage of which a tourist can take advantage without having to go through an inclusive travel website.

But these companies are still in the marketing game and even tourists not taking advantage of travel agencies and websites are still subjected to it. Rental car, hotel, and airline companies use a variety of mediums to advertise their goods and services. One of the biggest ways these companies reach their target audiences is through Internet marketing. This is a huge umbrella term, but in general, this means these companies are purchasing ad space and time from websites that they know their target audience is using. These ads sometimes, and even most often, are on websites that may have little or nothing to do with travel. The big indirect advertising movement that takes place everywhere on the Internet has proven to be a successful marketing technique. For example, say an airline company that specializes in short, local flights has completed research on their target audience to find out what extracurricular activities in which this group of people likes to participate. The airline company goes and buys ads on websites dedicated to those activities. Now anybody who likes those activities, and searches for websites linked to them online, will see these ads. Does this mean all of the people who see these ads will then go buy a flight on this airline? No. But it means that the company has done its research, and it knows that the people who take the most local flights in the areas they offer are highly connected also to particular activities. And now it has planted the idea of taking a flight on its airline in the minds of every one of these people, which increases the awareness of the company as well as ticket purchases. In other words, no doubt, these companies are doing their research and they are finding more and more customers every day through calculated, intentional marketing campaigns, whether the target of the ad is aware or not. Although it may appear to be so, there is not a lot of coincidence in the ads people see every day on the Internet.

Another way that these companies optimize marketing is through incentive programs. The use rate of incentive programs for businesses is soaring at record speeds. With the realization that existing customers cost less to reach than new ones, and provide long-term economic stability for them, businesses are taking advantage of this retention strategy as part of their marketing structures. By offering incentive programs, these businesses happily invite customers back and are increasing their return business by a huge margin. Especially in the travel industry where the goods or services cost much more than everyday items, the incentives are more valuable to a person in the long term. When the cost of living is going up and the prices of goods and services are so much higher than in decades past, an incentive program is presented as offering free goods and services, and it delivers.

When there is an incentive to gain points towards cheaper or even free travel in the future, it motivates the traveler in a very unique way. People see these programs as offering them free money. For a large amount of the population that travels, taking advantage of travel incentive programs from rental car companies, hotels, and airlines just makes sense. It encourages and increases the return customer count for the companies and gives back to the tourist at the same time. And the incentive program not only retains tourists, but it creates new ones. Now that the idea is prevalent with more major travel businesses, the competition is fierce. This means that these companies have to out-advertise each other in order to catch the attention of the tourist. That initial contact with the tourist is vital. Even if everybody is offering an incentive program, as long as the tourist is happy with the service of the first company he or she uses, there will not be a reason to switch. Incentive programs make lifelong customers and the advertising it costs to get them is worth it. Often, people plan out shopping specifically for the company with the better offer or incentive. This includes people looking at clothing stores, groceries, restaurants, hotels, or airline companies. Now that incentive programs are mainstream, you will often hear customers ask businesses about what incentives they offer. Incentives are no longer a new trend, but mainstream, and it is up to every company to jump on board.

LOCAL BUSINESSES

Other key players in the travel and tourism industry are the local businesses within a destination. As mentioned earlier in the chapter, the local businesses are a very special ingredient in the mix of the tourism industry. These are the businesses and the people that make the memories for the tourists once they arrive. They help to build the character of a city or nation, and they add to the physical and emotional experiences of the trip. Local businesses can include retail, hospitality, services, transit, and more. Think about the city in which you live, and all of the places you go for goods and services on a daily, weekly, and monthly basis. These are the places the tourists in your area will visit that will leave an impression of the region on them. These businesses, just like every single other part of the industry, also partake in marketing.

Local businesses are not always first encountered when entering an area. But sometimes the local businesses of cities and nations that are well immersed in the tourist area advertise on travel websites with agencies and through personal websites. The tourist who is organized might want to plan his or her meals and activities ahead of time for his or her trip. In this case, finding out about local restaurants and places to go ahead of time is key. By researching, this tourist is able to find places he or she wants to go, so when he or she arrives at the destination, he or she can easily find where he or she wants to go. In this case, it is in the best interest of local businesses to join the movement and advertise globally to tourists to become part of the tourist's agenda before the trip begins. Luckily, there are many ways they can do this. Sometimes this will come in the form of buying ads on the Internet like the big companies. But sometimes, this venue of advertising isn't the most feasible for small businesses. This being the case, a strategic marketing move for these small businesses is to create partnerships. Creating relationships with already-established businesses in the area that target tourists can help boost their images and businesses. By partnering with these businesses, a small business can be part of a tour package marketing plan. These tour packages, often involving multiple small businesses, have the capacity to advertise through the Internet, the biggest and most efficient way to reach the tourist directly. There are also websites that work directly with small businesses to help resell their packages, goods, or services in order to connect their customers, tourists, directly with local businesses.

Another way for small businesses to gain immediate attention from tourists is through making partnerships with bigger businesses and attractions that physically funnel tourists to them. For example, if a tourist is visiting one of the wonders of the world, a majority of the time he or she is going to ask the attraction's organized team where the best place is for lunch, dinner, or shopping. Small businesses that develop a relationship with these natural attractions are guaranteed that a percentage of the traffic ends up at their doorstep. Building relationships with local, state, and national governments as well as trade organizations is essential for these small businesses to enact their marketing strategies. These key connections bring industry leaders together with local businesses which are the heart of the industry. Taking advantage of these partnerships is absolutely essential for these local small businesses to successfully reach the tourist, the same as for any larger company. Also critical to their growth is the use of direct Internet marketing. The ability to appear at the top of search engine lists, whether being a small business or large company, is now realistic for an affordable price. By optimizing the Internet, and taking advantage of its power for advertising, small businesses can now optimize their chance of reaching tourists pre-arrival.

Another marketing tool that local businesses really thrive in using is physical advertising, used in almost every large tourist area. The effect of small local business owners handing a flyer to a tourist or talking to him or her about their businesses is fairly unparalleled to any other type of advertising. The advantage this type has over any other is the human element. Some are drawn to this more than others, but no matter what, this personal touch has an emotional pull to it far more than any other marketing attempts found on the Internet or in print. The tourist is able to directly interact with a person, ask questions, and connect with the local business. The persuasion of a personal invitation to use or go to a small business seems to be more irresistible than any other. People tend to believe in true, positive intents from a person more so than they do from a computer. With online marketing campaigns, the tourist is able to take his or her time, sift through information, and pick and choose by calculated methods where he or she wants to go and what he or she wants to do. But face to face, it makes it harder for the tourist to turn down an invitation to try something. The tourist is unable to slow down and think about options, or weigh the pros and cons. The small business has the upper hand in the personal advertising medium.

THE HOST COMMUNITY

The support and buy-in of the host community is vital in supporting a local tourism industry. When the local tourism authority is strategizing its plan for the region, taking into account the host community is an essential step to get it where they want to be economically within the tourism industry. Without the people driving the strategy in the right direction, a nation would, as nations have, fail in the global tourism business. Tourism can be a useful element in community enrichment, but it can also be a harmful business to the host community. The tourism authority of a city or nation must prioritize the effects of their decisions on the host community, who should be considered the region's most important natural resource. That is why it is so important that the two work together to make tourism a thriving part of the host community.

The interactions that happen between the tourist and local community can affect both the tourist and the locals strongly. The local community affects the delicate relationship the tourist is going to have with his or her destination either positively or negatively. The host community holds in its hands the power to create an unforgettable experience for the tourist, or leaving a lifelong impression on the tourist that it is not desirable. Both the tourist's unique culture and that of the host community can be either intriguing to one another or overwhelming and uncomfortable. The host community reaches out on a personal level to the tourist as any other part of the tourism chain does. But its unique one-on-one accessibility to the tourist is a relationship unlike any other. In a quick example, imagine you own a business. When you hire employees, you are carefully making sure each and every one of them can, and will, represent your business the way you want it represented at all times, whether you are there or, more importantly, when you are not. Without this seamless representation, even by just one employee, the business faces taking on a reputation that is not supported by your mission as the owner. The same scenario is true of the leaders in a city or nation for the tourism industry and the host community. If they are not all on the same page at all times, then the infrastructure will crack, leaving an unstable foundation for the tourism business of that destination.

Souvenirs are a huge part of the tourism industry, economically speaking, for a destination. It is the host community that often creates and shares the souvenirs that tourists crave. To be able to communicate with the local community and hear about and see the culture in a tangible way, firsthand, is priceless to tourists. And to be able to take a piece of that experience home with them to share with others and to remember for themselves the times they spent at their destinations creates one of the biggest emotional ties people have with local cultures and with destinations on a whole.

The marketing techniques that the host community uses are personal and physical. Their opportunities to advertise lie simply in the one-on-one arena, far from any electronic or global tool. This is not to say that there is no competition in the local community's sales of local and cultural goods. If you have ever visited marketplaces in large tourist areas, you know how overwhelming the local merchants' areas can be. To the host community that depends of these sales for its livelihood, the opportunity to interact and sell goods and services to the tourists coming into its homeland is vital to survival. If not by assumption, then by probability, the tourist has the economic ability to pay whatever it is the host community is asking of him or her for its goods and services. The prices of items presented by a local community are often derived from a low-cost point, which means its opportunity to raise the margin lies in its ability to communicate with the tourist. The competition from one vendor to another can even be cutthroat, with prices and offers being thrown about to the tourist. It is the side of marketing the tourist never sees when shopping on the Internet, sifting through competitive deals.

This is not to say the host community is not happy to be part of the industry. Although there are often vital circumstances around the success of its sales, the host community can also be overwhelmingly happy to share its culture with a tourist. The sale may be the bottom line, but the vendors in the host community are opening their land, offering their hard work, and sharing their culture with the tourist, leaving an impression that will never be forgotten.

BRANDING: CITIES AND NATIONS

City and nation tourism authorities are the managers of the tourism industry, creating business strategies targeted to reach their goals just like any other business. But the other thing they also do, just like any other business would attempt, is try to create a brand for their destinations. Today, one of the many types of branding is nation branding. A nation brand is one, if not the most, necessary part of its business and marketing plan. The branding of a nation is necessary to not only build and manage a destination's image and reputation in the eyes of the tourist, but in the eyes of the world. It is done to raise awareness of a destination's distinctive characteristics in order to appeal to a wide audience of tourists. A majority of nations have a separate resource set aside dedicated to building and improving the brand of their nations. A destination's standing in the global view is vital to its success rate in attracting new tourists and welcoming back repeat visitors. Of course, the bottom line of branding is the effect it has on the economic growth of a location.

To put in perspective the importance of a nation brand, compare it to the branding of a goods company. For example, think about the products purchased on a daily basis in the world and the places from which they are purchased. Could you imagine Levi Strauss jeans or McDonald's being successful without their consistent and relevant advertisements? Companies selling products and corporations opening businesses across the world would never consider not having a brand for their products and businesses. It is an automatic requirement for companies to build their brands. And they are not the only ones acknowledging that building a brand is vital to their successes. Some of the best-branded products and companies in the world are those that have created logos, with or without words, are recognized around the globe, not restrained by language or cultural barriers. For instance, think of the Starbucks logo. If you saw that logo, would you need any written information to tell you for whom the logo was? Most people would not! They would automatically recognize that logo, anywhere in the world, and know that it stood for Starbucks. That scenario is the goal of all branding, whether for a product, business, or location.

The term *personal branding* has become extremely popular as people realized they could market themselves and their careers as brands. It started from the foundation that it is important in today's competitive world to create an image for oneself, something to sell along with one's many talents. The human mind can only take in so much information from so many places. In order for people to stand out, for products to stand out among millions, for businesses to attract customers, and for cities and nations to pull tourists to their destinations, a thoughtful, well-calculated, attractive brand must be created to lure in attention.

Smaller and, often, developing countries strive to create brands for themselves not only for attracting tourists, but to carry heavier weight in the global view and political relations. Nations are branding themselves not only in efforts for a tourism strategy, but in their attempts to be seen in a particular light by the world. The business of branding is just like any other business with which tourism authorities work. Cities and nations alike hire public relations firms and marketing companies in order to assist them in building their brands. Some nations spend millions of U.S. dollars contracting projects to these firms to build their brands. These firms create relationships with the target markets, gather information, analyze data, and create information that is then presented to the client cities or nations. Although there are tangible elements to the tourism business, it is the intangible elements of the locations that are important to highlight. The experience that the city or nation offers and the impression it leaves on the tourist are big parts in branding management. Branding offers a nation a connection between itself and a positive emotional perception of a tourist for the purpose of pulling him or her toward itself over another destination. It uses positive images and creates a strong awareness of its location, building a strong tourist base.

The terms *nation branding* and *city branding* specifically refer to the use of corporate branding techniques for cities and nations. There is a very fine line that separates pieces of the process of the new form of nation branding from public diplomacy. Nations now are far more aware of the value of their brands as assets. By understanding this, nations understand what weight their actions and investments have on their images. This is causing nations to further invest in their images and branding. Nations are now conscious that all of the messages they send out on every level are bouncing back and provide a representation of their views and the fundamental common purposes of their countries. The branding of nations has become a more sophisticated means of attracting tourists over some other forms of advertising and is also used to lure in foreign investments, secure geopolitical influence, and even facilitate global trade. Nations are taking branding to another level, attempting to attract the good graces of not just the tourist, but other countries.

Although there are polls and firms working to quantify the effect that branding has on nations, there is still not a consistent and accurate way to directly connect branding efforts to global economic growth. What can be measured is the overall growth or decline in each individual city or nation making attempts at branding. When numbers are gathered before and during a branding campaign, destinations are able to better understand if what they are doing is working or not. This means that the branding can and has affected cities and states positively and negatively. An effort to create an image of a city or nation in one light can quickly and deeply destroy its standing in the tourism business. For example, there is a big question about this branding epidemic as to whether or not nations are using branding as smoke and mirrors in an effort to hide their not-so-pleasant parts from global view. In other words, they are using branding to cover up bad policy with good public relations. When this happens, and a nation brands itself with a false, optimistic image despite the world being aware of the negative political turmoil behind the scenes, it could off-put tourists from wanting to travel to that destination out of concern that it is misrepresenting itself.

But branding can take time. It is not a quick-fix effort to cover up a country's turmoil or rapidly gain an enormous tourist attraction over one season. It is a delicate process with as many working parts in its strategy as there are in any other business strategy. The process also requires the full attention and buy-in from the destination's government leaders as well as the private-sector heads. It is a partnership between these groups with the firm or outside agency brought in to create the brand. Every single person in the process must be on the same page. When a brand is created, it has to carry the same theme throughout the country. That means that the tourism board, the host community, the local businesses, politicians, and the investment-promotion boards say the same thing about the nation that's in conjunction with the nation's theme and brand. Without support holding up the brand from all angles, it will fail.

LAS VEGAS, NEVADA, USA

Las Vegas, Nevada and its branding decisions are a perfect example how it can be successful to embrace what a destination is and not try to create an image of what a destination clearly is not. It was able to break out of the branding mold of pretty pictures and guarantees of good times to paint a picture of what it was offering really to its visitors. It went after the brand-technique that grabbed the emotions of the tourist to create a connection between him or her and its destination. The campaign upon which it embarked wrapped its ideas justly around what its brand meant, to live in the hearts and minds of the consumers.

Its campaign started by gathering information. In order to analyze and make decisions accurately, one needs to collect data in order to offer useful decisions. That is when Las Vegas stumbled upon the essence of its location from the perspective of the tourist. On a regular basis during research, tourists revealed that they felt they could cut loose in Vegas like nowhere else, without any worries. This idea led the tourism board down the road that its destination meant "adult freedom" in a nutshell. By embracing what actually happens in the city, the truth behind a lot of tourist agendas, they were able to create a brand and ad campaign that reflected it to its core. The city was already known as being provocative and edgy. The "What Happens Here" campaign just made the secret an open invitation to join in the fun.

In order for a brand to be successful, it needs to provide the truth about what the destination offers as an experience, not just as a sum of goods and services. A perfect example of this is when some Las Vegas hotels started marketing the city as a family destination. They built theme parks and water parks on their resort properties in attempts to convince the public that Vegas was the destination for their family fun vacations. Clearly, this campaign did not embrace the true essence of the city and therefore could not convince tourists to visit with that idea in mind. The campaigns failed, needless to say, as the local tourism authority would not support them, and thankfully so. Las Vegas ranks as one of the top powerful city brands in the world on a list of other impressive destinations. Their upbeat, catchy, edgy, and appropriately updated brand "What happens in Vegas, stays in Vegas" has caught the global eye of tourists looking for more than a good time.

CANADA

Canada has ranked as one of the top-branded countries in the world for years. Their campaign "Canada. Keep exploring." truly captures its strong sense of place as well as its inviting community and authentic personality. In the tag line alone, it invites tourists to see Canada as a destination that offers exploration. Canada has successfully branded itself as a place of natural beauty and welcoming people. When we talk about the value of an experience, Canada is a perfect example of a destination that has invested itself in that tenfold.

Canada's place has been consistent over the years on lists of global rankings, including Futurebrand, the world's leading branding firm in strategy, design, and innovation. They help people and businesses make decisions about the future, using brands as a guide. They define a brand of the future as one that helps people compromise between what they think and how they feel. In other words, decisions that only affect the short term or those that will positively dictate the long term. Their country brand index rankings measure global perceptions across several dimensions including tourism, exports, and culture. What better way to make decisions than by predicting the future? That is exactly what the Country Brand Index (CBI) does.

But interestingly enough, even with Canada's high global rankings, an independent firm called Studio 360 felt that Canada needed rebranding. The project began in 2012 when they felt the country's reputation was stuck in a quicksand of clichés. In particular, the country's closest neighbor, the United States, had a very poor level of understanding and knowledge of them. They felt that what Canada really needed was not a rebrand or redesign, but the opportunity to educate the world about the true Canada. Hence, their pitch: Know Canada. They used one of the most effective streams of communication by tapping into the app market. By letting users be part of the visual redesign of the country, they were able to personally connect with Canada. The app let users put whatever picture they wanted between the country's flag's two red stripes to express how they saw Canada. And although the visual redesign testing was successful, the project still remained speculative. Canada was aware of the project but decided to stick to its strong, resilient brand. It has a very specific set of guidelines that outlines the various expressions of the nation's brand. But having reached hundreds of thousands of people through Studio 360's challenge, the theoretical redesign of the country quite possibly altered the perceptions of the nation, especially having a positive direct effect on its southern neighbors in the United States, one of the original motivations.

PARIS

When it comes to the ranking of global city images, Paris has been affixed at the top almost unchallenged. The city's brand "City of Light" is supported by a global cultural icon and the most recognizable structure in the world, the Eiffel Tower. It is a city that has capitalized on the selling of its history, lifestyle, diversity, food, and quality of place. Its efforts in forming relationships consistently with city municipalities and government bodies in order to enhance its visibility and infrastructure has aided in keeping it at the top of the most-visited destinations in the world. In terms of city brand rankings by the Anholt-GfK City Brands Index (CBISM), which measures the power and appeal of each city's brand image, Paris has been on top for many years. Just as the Futurebrand Country Brand Index compares top nations, the CBISM provides a holistic perspective of cities, looking at key dimensions: presence (the city's international status and standing), place (its physical aspect), prerequisites (basic requirements, such as affordable accommodations and the standard of public amenities), people, pulse (interesting things to do), and potential (economic and educational opportunities).

Paris has been able to market itself almost naturally, riding on its long-term engrained reputation as a city of romance. Although the romantic images of Paris may be clichés, they prove to be strong global attractions to the romantic tourist. The experiences Paris provides for romance are endless. The city has capitalized on its romantic characteristics such as the Eiffel Tower, the Seine, and the theatre, and it can guarantee an unforgettable experience for its tourists every single time. But even though it is the irresistible city of romance, Paris has also maintained a reputation of being rude to its tourists. In 2013, there was an inner-city campaign launched in order to re-train its host community on how to communicate appropriately with tourists. A manual was created, *Do you speak Touriste?*, which included greetings in multiple languages as well as tips on cultural codes and the spending habits of various cultures. The campaign targeted taxi drivers, hospitality workers, and retail employees. The Paris Chamber of Commerce has been long aware of their city's reputation and equally aware that their city, one of the most visited by tourists in the world, has competition on the horizon, forcing them to tidy up their unwelcoming behavior.

GREECE

Greece is a country that has been in the top ranks for beaches, night life, food, scenery, and overall positive place to visit for a holiday. Its history, heritage, art, and culture have been natural lures for tourists over the decades; it is always a unique and welcoming stop in the European zone. It also has been rated as one of the most romantic places visited by tourists, with seaside villages and walkable cities. The country has always prioritized its tourism sector, knowing that it is one of the staples of its economy. And although from a tourist point of view the country was a desirable destination, what tourists did not see for decades was the turmoil bubbling behind the scenes of the country. For decades the country ran poorly in the area of administration, which became one of the greatest failures of Greek democracy today. Choices of successive governments paid little attention to financial matters, such as putting together a tax collection service in order to provide the country with sufficient economic resources in the future and distribute the tax burden through impartial methods. What tourists may have not known about Greece is that from 1999 to 2007, French and German banks poured money into the country, bending over backward to lend Greece funds. The over-lending easily led to overspending and their first bailout in 2010. Although some pointed fingers at Greece in blame, the bailout was more for its creditor banks, not the Greek state. The disorder continued with another bailout in 2012, clearly a sign that there had not been any more attention given to the necessary factors within Greece to make changes in its infrastructure. It was not until

2015 that Greece was put on the map, not as a top tourist destination, but as a country that was broke.

The current state of Greece has dramatically changed its brand in the eyes of tourists and its image in the eyes of the world. Although nobody can pinpoint exactly whom to blame for its situation, the fact is that it cannot erase what has happened. Tourists immediately began to pull back when the country announced there was a limit on how much money could be withdrawn from their on a daily basis. Sometimes when a brand goes bad there is no return. But Greece's people and culture are not to blame for its current financial troubles. Unfortunately, explaining to tourists that it's not their fault is not a viable way to regain its image. While some tourists follow the news and take in all of the information regarding situations like this, many tourists assume the destination is no longer good, and have marked it off their lists. Only time can tell if a brand can be rejuvenated.

QATAR

Some cities and nations do not have as much natural ability to attract tourists. Destinations like Qatar have to work hard around the clock to create a strategic marketing plan and stick to it. Luckily for Qatar, it has proven it can do it. From 2009 to 2014, the amount of foreign tourists visiting Qatar increased an astonishing 91%. For a place where the tourism industry did not exist ten years ago, it has made leaps and bounds towards attracting tourists and in 2013 reached a 1.3 million count in foreign visitors. By vigorously marketing itself as a luxurious travel destination, and introducing events, medical services, and tourism products, it has come well up to par globally with other popular tourist destinations. And this growth is still not at the peak at which the nation prefers to be functioning. Qatar worked hard and won the bid to be the 2022 World Cup location, opening up opportunities in its tourism industry as well as generating local and global investments. Qatar has set the bar even higher, striving to continue increasing tourists' visits with a goal of seven million visitors a year by 2030.

Up until 2008, oil-dependent countries in the Middle East carried similar political economic structures, and were not part of any tourism planning. Traditionally, tourism was culturally unwelcome and economically needless. But in order to counter the effect of decreasing oil revenue and increased population, Qatar and other similar nations turned to the potential market of tourism. But this meant these countries' branding strategies did not have a lot of research to reference. Unlike many other nations, Qatar is just recently building its tourism strategy and writing its own history. But this is one of the benefits for the location. They have been able to create their own agenda with the tourism authority without being stuck in an old rut that's not there. Qatar's fresh, new take on tourism is all the better with modern technologies. What they do have to go on is the history of tourism in general. They are able to bypass all of the ideas that have failed destinations all over the world and come up with ones that work. Qatar has hit a gold mine in terms of their grasp on tourism.

To build its sustainability over a long period of time, Qatar has chosen to focus on what tourism calls the three S's of tourism: sand, sea, and sun. But realizing it needs to expand its appeal in order to gain a sharper increase of tourist traffic, it has added additional focuses: shopping, medicine, sports, education, safari, and skyscrapers; and are also taking advantage of industries including meetings, incentives, conferences, and exhibitions (MICE) as well as culture. In order to gain a competitive edge over other destinations, including a neighbor competitor, Dubai, Qatar must diversify its strategy. Qatar has also had international support in its venture to join the international ranks of competitive tourist destinations. In a call to update the list of the Wonders of the World, a foundation, New7Wonders, presented a global vote in 2014. The results landed Doha, Qatar on the list as one of the new seven wonder cities in the world. With the country's increasing, persistent efforts to form a global view of itself as a prominent figure in tourism, Qatar is quickly gaining unstoppable momentum to not only push the tourism industry to the top of its economic stability, but to push the envelope as one of the most visited destinations in the world.

RUSSIA

Russia is the largest country in the world, containing almost a dozen time zones and bordered by fourteen other countries whose inhabitants speak more than 100 languages and dialects. Its economic power lies with its natural resources of oil, natural gas, metals, and timber. The government, semi-authoritative, owns or runs most of the nation's mass media outlets. Russia clearly lacks a solid national identity, leaving it at the bottom of every ranking in terms of nation brand, with no national tourism campaign. Although rich in culture and unparalleled in size, Russia has many forces working against it for creating a national brand. In fact, all of the hard facts about the country highlight its challenge to creating a consistent image across the mass of land and people. It covers more than 6.6 million square miles, but with a less-dense population than some smaller countries. This means that people are even further spread out, bringing everybody together on the same page nearly impossible.

But there are big occurrences that can potentially bring good luck to a country without a national image; for example, the 2014 Winter Olympics in Sochi, Russia. Although the global events held in Sochi strengthened and motivated the region to pursue Russia as an attractive tourist destination, there was not a drastic change in the teamwork of the country towards common marketing and image strategies. The glimpse the world did receive of Russia through Sochi did help to positively influence its view of the country and the people, but not enough to magically create a top tourist destination overnight. Branding requires the efforts of many working parts and can take still, in all organized efforts, years to create an image and set an impression into global minds.

Russia has such a rich history and a list of desirable assets, including its abundance of natural resources, a large educated workforce, and high levels of investment with the global financial market. But unfortunately, it has currently stronger forces working against it. Its elite-controlled political power, inner corruption, censorship laws, and highly underdeveloped legal system hold it back from a nationwide transformation into a modern powerhouse. Without a more cohesive effort and major structural changes, Russia will not be keeping up domestically or internationally when it comes to desirable tourist destinations.

SHANGHAI

Not only is Shanghai the largest Chinese city by population, but it is also the largest city by population in the world. It is home to the world's busiest container port and is one of the biggest global transportation hubs. By history a center of commerce between the East and West, and although experiencing ups and downs, Shanghai has come out ahead, regaining its reputation. In most recent years, Shanghai has been hailed as one of the fastest-growing cities in the world. The city was the location of the 2010 World Expo, which became a pivotal event for the country to demonstrate that Shanghai was an attractive, modern, and comfortable city infused with traditional Chinese values and ready to compete for talent and investments with other global cities. China, the world's second-largest economy, has had an ongoing strategy to develop Shanghai into one of the world's leading financial and commercial centers. The 2010 Expo was branded "Better City, Better Life" and pushed Shanghai toward that goal. World expos have provided undeniable assists to transform destinations, presenting notions of progress and sustainability to global audiences. Shanghai, naturally equipped with a blend of cultures and nationalities as well as financial responsibility for its country, was the perfect city to host the World Expo and enhance its own image.

"More discovery, more experience," has kept Shanghai on the map as a top tourist destination. It has embraced, and marketed itself, as being a melting pot of cultures. That multicultural flair and its combinations of modern and traditional as well as western and oriental is attractive to tourists from all over the world. It promotes its own culture as one that has intertwined western customs with Chinese traditions. The only setback the city has to overcome, if it ever will, is air pollution. When China pushed the slogan "Beautiful China," endless news articles and videos sank the notion that the country is completely beautiful. The pollution problem that Shanghai has is an example of a chemical problem that is out of the destination's hands. But luckily, Shanghai has built an empire of attraction with its history and booming cultural offerings, outweighing the gray skies, which let them continue to grow its numbers of inbound tourists. As such a large, globally influential city, it will take more than air pollution to hold back its growth.

EVENTS AND TOURISM

History dictates that events play a huge role in the tourism industry. The role and importance of international events and their significance to the tourism business should not be underestimated. The events themselves bring awareness of destinations to the global audience. Whether or not a tourist visits during an event, an event still puts a location on the map of positive recognition. And mega-events, such as Olympics and World Expos, tend to promote locations as progressive, relatable cities and nations. They bring the human touch to locations that were considered possibly unvisitable or daunting to explore before the event. And still other events, such as meetings and conferences, play parts in the perception of a destination. Any event that draws people in to a location sparks some interest that was not there before. That's not to write that there are not negative ripple effects on a destination from the viewpoint of the host community and natural habitat, especially with larger events. But is there a balance or a choice between fueling the tourism business and preserving the health and safety of the local community when hosting an event? That depends of the destination and its priorities.

MICE: MEETINGS, INCENTIVES, CONFERENCES, EXHIBITIONS

MICE (meetings, incentives, conferences, and exhibitions) is a distinct type of tourism in which organized large groups come together for a common, specific purpose. Also known as the meetings industry, it is a consistent occurrence of well-planned agendas centered on a theme and attended by a special interest group or businesses and organizations with a common goal. The locations chosen for these meetings are often voted upon by the bigger businesses involved in the event or a specialized convention group. And it's no surprise that destinations promote their locations to the meetings industry. Marketing plays just as big of a role within the meetings industry as it does in the larger scope of the tourism business. Cities are bidding on big and small events in the meetings industry, using it is as another avenue to secure global recognition as tourist-equipped locations.

The acronym MICE clarifies what makes up the meetings industry. *Meetings* is a general word to indicate the gathering of a group of people with the same agenda. Incentives are meeting events that is part of a program that offers rewards for past performance. This differs most from the others, but with incentive programs soaring, it is still a vital piece of the industry. Conferences are participatory meetings held for discussions pertaining to problem solving, education, and consultation. Smaller in nature than other events in the meetings industry, the format is purposefully designed for the sharing of information among a group. Being small in size tends to facilitate the goal to address specific objectives much easier. Exhibitions are events where products and services are displayed.

Cities and nations are becoming more aware of the meetings industry and its growing niche in the tourism business. In general, as transportation and travel become more accessible, it is not only the tourist on holiday who is visiting international destinations more regularly; the business world is using foreign destinations to set a standard of professionalism when planning events. There is one big difference between the tourist traveling for personal motivations and the business tourist. Those traveling for business have much higher expectations than the everyday traveler. In order to maintain a consistent professional environment, businesses and event planners are looking for locations with a professional vibe that can uphold the image of their events. Meetings require an inclusive destination, offering easy access to accommodations, catering, meeting facilities, transportation, entertainment, technology, and sometimes special venues. In order for them to present a packaged event, they need to be able to secure the necessities they require at their destinations.

Even though business tourists require a more developed destination to create appeal and professionalism, a destination has a very unique advantage when opening its door to the business tourist. With there being a sharp increase in tourists mixing business travel and leisure travel together, meetings destinations should be able to convert these event travelers into leisure tourists. With the ability to extend their stays at a destination beyond their business agendas, business travelers are often looking to spend a few extra days in their destinations for leisure. So by spending the extra time to build an atmosphere that attracts and welcomes meetings and events, a destination is at the same time increasing the number of inbound tourists, developing a better tourism infrastructure, and enhancing its tourism economy. In other words, business destinations provide a two-for-one experience for the tourist and quite possibly double the profit for the destination. It also helps that business tourists tend to spend more money at their events destination than leisure travelers and more often in a shorter period of time.

But still there are the bigger events that land at a destination due to a far more complicated marketing and planning system.

Events such as the Olympics, World Expo, World Cup, and many others, begin their planning far in advance. And by far in advance, that means at least several years. Boards and organization leaders begin their search for a destination up to a decade in advance to begin narrowing down the field of possible locations. There are so many levels of qualifications a destination must have, specific to the event, in order to be short-listed as a possibility. But even then, how do the event planners know they can depend on that destination to offer at the event what they are attracted to now? In other words, what's to say that a natural disaster or political instability won't affect the destination before the event? In order to make the best-educated decision, there are many lines of defense that go before the choosing of the destination. History provides a solid foundation for determining if the location is a viable choice, and the marketing campaigns direct from the destination also provide a solid picture.

If there is any possibility for a city or nation to be considered for a mega-international event, you'd better believe that they are pulling out all of the tricks to compete. With a chance to physically attract thousands, and in some cases hundreds of thousands, of tourists to a region in a short period of time, all efforts must be on board. Not only do these large events attract huge numbers of visitors, but with the help of the media, social and otherwise, the city or nation is exposing itself for the entire world to see what it has to offer. So not only is it affected by the inbound tourists during the event, but by the buzz created during the time leading up to the event and to the residual effect after it. A world event can change a city or nation forever, and has in the past. The lifetime opportunity a pivotal global event brings to a destination is priceless.

As previously mentioned, cities and nations around the world are hard at work creating marketing campaign strategies on an ongoing basis to attract tourists to their destinations. But what most do not realize is that destinations are in constant bidding competitions to host mega events. To do this, the city not only has to have a solid global marketing campaign alive and well in the tourism economy, but a separate marketing plan just for that event. Again, it is double work, and double hard, but most profitable if successful. Once it successfully lands an event, a location's work continues up a steep climb. It is the responsibility of a city and a nation to protect their host communities and environments when taking on events of a large caliber. The effects of an international event are similar to the effects large amounts of tourism have on a host community, but on a larger scale. Jobs and the guarantee of financial success are created, but lives are also directly affected. Oftentimes to build the arenas necessary to facilitate a global event, homes are torn down or moved, the natural habitat can be transformed into flat land for building, and the onslaught of people can bring pollution and decimation of an area. This is why a bid for a global event is not just to bring in numbers of people to an area. A bid to host an international event is a commitment to the event, to the world, to the nation, and to the local community. An international event can bring the world together and it is the destination's obligation to do so responsibly.

Part Four
Tourism behind the Scenes

Have you ever wondered what happens on the set of a movie? Or how the special effects were created for an onstage production? The idea of looking behind the scenes is a trending subject that is gaining momentum and expanding in depth. Think about all of the television shows and magazines and Internet websites providing a sneak peak behind the scenes and into the real lives of celebrities. The curiosity of the consumer is turning into a feeling of privilege because of the unlimited access to all of this once forbidden information. It would be a tall order to try to keep track of how many media outlets provided this information.

What about behind the scenes of the tourism industry? This sector has just as many secrets when the tourist is looking the other way, in order to maintain an overall happy and catering environment. And as for comparing it to a movie set: That's spot on. The elaborate planning, organizing, and theme building behind the scenes at tourism and hospitality businesses are all too similar to what goes on at entertainment businesses. But that's the job of a service-oriented business: to create an experience that immediately transports the consumer to an environment outside of his or her stress-filled everyday life. Service can be defined as the action or process of serving food, drinks, and other goods to customers but it can also mean a system of supplying a need, the action of helping, and the action of creating an intangible experience. The tourism industry itself is categorized as an experience business, which allows it to add opportunities to reach customers, and provide memorable encounters with its goods and services.

If you are a consumer as described above, privy to information about celebrities, then you know that a behind-the-scenes glimpse provides more than just the fame and glamour snapshot of their lives. The same goes for tourism and hospitality. On the outside, in view of the consumer, the service industry is a stage prepped for every possible interaction and occurrence with a presentation of ease. But there are a number of uncontrollable variables playing devil's advocate daily against the team on the stage as well as the team putting together and managing the business aspects of these companies. And even deeper into the businesses under the service industry umbrella are lingering cultural issues and stereotypes with a solid history of negative connotations. But all in all, most would be amazed at the infrastructure of the businesses behind the scenes in what most key players know as the experience industry.

THE EXPERIENCE

It would be unfair to write about behind the scenes of the tourism industry without mentioning some of the most important pieces to the business's structures such as transportation, accommodations, retail, entertainment, and others. Experience marketing is not a new concept, but it is a growing one, and is the core of the most successful global businesses, within and beyond the tourism industry. It has been coined with the term *the experience industry* for its direct focus on providing an experience. When a business uses experience design, it is focusing on designing goods, services, environments, and events based on the quality of the tourist experience. This approach stems from studies and research in cognitive and perceptual psychology, environmental design, brand strategy, storytelling, service design, and product design to name a few. In the tourism industry, this design is driven by the engagement between people and their goods or services and the ideas, emotions, and memories that these "touchpoints" create. Touchpoints describe the interface of a service, or product, with the customer, the tourist, before the transaction takes place. Studying these touchpoints helps the business to optimize the impact of their efforts. Since transactions take place across a variety of media and channels, a focus on each of the touchpoints accompanied by an assessment and systematic management plan can lead a business to an impact-oriented experience and an improvement of the overall brand or service perception, essentially leading to more transactions.

When we refer to experience design, it is not far off from the concept of brand marketing. Situations, experiences, interactions, and data are all being analyzed and utilized to create a stronger connection between the consumer, the tourist, and the goods and services, or destination.And as in all businesses, in the tourism industry the businesses taking part of this design are also crafting the experience *for* the employees and *with* the employees and every other person involved in the business that interacts with the tourist. When an experience is designed and activated, from that point on, every person who comes within the parameters set for the experience is playing a role in the design. Sometimes this involves just the business and its staff as well as customers, and sometimes others wander onto the stage who are not even aware of the business directly. These people play the parts of unknown variables, which is within the category of uncontrollable variables that management has to systematically deal with on a daily basis in order to maintain the flow of the experience.

Although this could fall into the marketing discussion previously mentioned, there is one big difference between experience marketing and traditional marketing. Although the two can be used in conjunction with one another effectively, they come from two different thoughts. Traditional marketing involves putting out advertisements across a wide media range to spread the word about a business and its function related to the consumer. But experience marketing is the personal touch to the traditional line of advertising. It focuses on the experiences and emotions of the customer, allowing the consumer to take ownership of the goods or services related to that marketing outreach because he or she has now an emotional connection to the product. He or she has a reason to remember the product; hopefully for the business, this will equate to the spreading by word of mouth to the customer's friends. And although marketing takes place every time a consumer comes in contact with that business through an ad, experience pertains to the senses, the full, physical contact with the goods or services.

The general population is aware that companies use marketing strategies to target it to buy their goods and services. But experience marketing falls under the behind-the-scenes umbrella of a tourism business because it is an intangible design and plan that is taken for granted by the naked eye. The environment, and every single detail in it, is often overlooked by the tourist in a hotel or at a restaurant. These designs are meant to be overlooked, to create a sensory environment and experience to make the tourist feel drawn to their goods and services. In other words, these businesses are working hard so the consumer doesn't notice that they're hard at work. It's hard work to create an experience that has the feeling of being natural.

Unfortunately, this method is just beyond the grasp of many businesses. Regardless of the business sector—service, retail, even manufacturing—businesses all have the ability to create an experience or an environment that even standing alone without the service or good in sight would create a lingering memory in the minds of the consumer. The main players in the service/tourism industry are hotels, restaurants, bars/nightclubs, theme parks, transportation, attractions, retail, and entertainment. And although there are other service-oriented businesses in play in the tourism market like consultants, information technology businesses, and event planners, these are the main business types that are working hard behind the scenes to bring an experience worthwhile to the consumer at their destination.

The design experience is a memorable sensory experience a business creates for its customers to create a direct link between the experience and the services or goods the business provides. Of course, a consumer has an experience every time he or she interacts with a business. But when a business sees the term as a direct call to action instead of an indirect action, there is a huge benefit for it. For example, if you had the power to make someone's experience in your presence positive and enjoyable instead of throwing all caution to the wind and just hoping it is, wouldn't you do it? Common sense tells us that of course you would! Why wouldn't we take advantage of molding that experience to yield exactly the reaction we desire? Unfortunately for some businesses, that type of common sense is overridden by other things. The time and effort required to create that experience does not fit into their budgets, calendars, or their limits to common-sense marketing. But it is fortunate for those that do take advantage of this golden opportunity.

Mistakenly, the terms *service* and *experience* have been used interchangeably. Although closely intertwined, they represent separate parts of a system. Services are intangible activities customized to the individual consumer's requests. Without the burden of maintaining stock on a good, service providers are free to invest in their expertise and focus all efforts towards tailoring their services to the consumer. An experience is something that the service provider, or any business, creates to engage the consumer fully, and enhance a positive connection to its services or goods. There are many schools of thought on exactly when this experience starts for a business. But to be genuinely a business that offers an invaluable experience for the consumer starts in the foundation, behind the scenes, during the marketing strategy and business plan drafting.

There are many steps a business must take to start running beyond functionality in order to compete on the basis of providing an experience. By adding in the depth of a designed experience with the simple function of a product, a business is raising the value of its product. An experience, positive or negative, has the natural capability to be passively absorbed through the senses of a consumer. For example, imagine walking into a hotel you booked online from a site that guaranteed the lowest prices and best service available. Comfortable that the hotel would provide all of the necessities, you arrive at the hotel with reasonable expectations. There is no valet, so you park your car in the first spot you find, which is a long walk to the lobby. So you don't have to walk back to the car, you bring all of your family's luggage with you to the lobby, where there is no concierge to open the door. Once inside, you see the bell desk with an employee sitting in a chair, texting on his cell phone. Nobody has greeted you or your family, so you leave them in the lobby and proceed to the front desk. There are two hotel clerks talking about where they went out the night before. As you continue to stand at the front desk, neither of them breaks his conversation to greet you. At this point, your heart is racing and your temper is fuming. You politely ask for their attention, and before turning to acknowledge you, they finish their sentences with each other first.

Any positive expectations you had of this hotel are completely gone, with no turn-around effect in sight. Already the business has not met your fundamental expectations of common courtesy, not to mention your expectations of above and beyond service from a service-oriented business! But you've already booked this non-refundable hotel, you're here at that hotel, and there's no turning back or changes to make in your plans at this point. Without going forward, let's just say the rest of the hotel visit is equally unsatisfying.

Now imagine the opposite. You drive up to a hotel you booked online that guaranteed the best price and excellent service. There is a valet who immediately acknowledges you with a wave and a smile. As you get out of the car, the valet calls over a bell service person to unload your bags onto a cart. When you tell them you are a few hours early, they still happily take all of your luggage, offering to keep it in a secure location until the room is ready. When your family walks into the lobby, it is a cool, refreshing temperature to battle the heat outside. Your family disperses immediately, since there are eye-catching activities all around. A table covered with snacks, ice water, and fresh coffee pulls you in one direction. The staff is spread out through the lobby to assist your with your questions about the property and area with inviting smiles, and there is a line of smiling faces behind the front desk, ample in number, able to move the guests through the check-in line with ease. Although your room isn't ready upon arrival, the desk clerk offers you vouchers for a discounted meal in one of their restaurants and suggests many activities to pass the time, along with the reassurance that the room will be available before check-in time and you will receive a personal call to let you know when your bags are in your room.

Both situations are lingering experiences in your mind. Once you have experienced both types of situations, you will agree that extraordinary experiences both positive and negative remain in your mind. The positive experience was crafted by the business, not a result of a simple action or gimmick. When a business provides this type of positive experience, it is because of a conscious choice it made to provide it. Successful companies in the tourism industry have adopted a policy of experience creation to maintain a competitive edge.

Technology is playing a bigger and bigger role in the experience design as innovation surges year after year. With the line between digital and analog experiences and online and offline experiences becoming seamless, it is often difficult to make a relative distinction between them, and it is becoming also irrelevant to do so. Technology is constantly evolving and becoming the enabler for people to live in and interact with the world around them at every level, including in the tourism industry. This evolution is changing the expectations, desires, and motivations of tourists, creating a higher demand for experiences with their goods and services. Technology is providing overwhelming solutions to problems we didn't even know we had. In other words, it is important for tourism businesses to maintain a human touch to their experiences, and remember the importance of creating experiences tied to the physical world. The bottom line of the experience industry is to make the experience count, take the time to research, tailor the experience to the tourist, and not to rely on technology to provide all of the environment. The number-one rule in customer service is that the customer comes first. It's that simple. Focus on pleasing the customer and creating a lasting bond between his or her experience and the good or service at hand.

With the connection terms like *design experience*, also known as *XD*, and *experience marketing* have with the super-speed of technological advances, one would think this market is new to the world. But on the contrary, the experience industry was ignited long before cell phones, the Internet, electronic advertising, and laptops. The man most directly pointed to in awe for his invention and creation of the 3D experience industry is Walt Disney. He was the first person to design and run a theme park. By adding extra layers of experiences for the guests on top of the structural amusement park foundation, he was able to evolve rides, food, and events into a new dimension of extreme experience. He created a story for his guests from before arrival to after departure. He set himself apart from the rest of the world for his time and today. The business that began it all continues to forge ahead of modern businesses, blazing a trail that most tourism businesses aspire to follow.

Imagine what it would be like if all businesses were set up this way. Shopping in a food market or running errands for household goods during your limited downtime would become anticipated adventures. People would look forward to all of their outings as if they were attending an entertainment show, but without the heavy ticket price attached. The dread of waiting in line at a store would transform into a full sensory experience. But the real question is, why aren't they? The foolproof plan has been set in place and all a business has to do is tweak it to its goods or services or target markets. Instead, businesses struggle to stay open and keep up with competitors, and refuse to use the data and resources at their fingertips. Some are naturally confined to a world in which things are the way they are and the business structure cannot be changed. If only they would follow the unique and successful plan of Disney. This is the dividing line between Disney and the companies that do not partake in experience businesses.

BUSINESS COMPONENTS

There are many moving parts behind the scenes of a tourism business. Every position and every detail of the business will have an effect on the tourist. But there are four major components that interact with one another that truly create the experience for all players involved. These components are the product or service, the customer, staff and management, and operations. To create a seamless experience for the tourist, three of these components must be first seamlessly structured from behind the curtain in order to interact precisely with the fourth component, the customer. One factor could not exist without the others in a tourist business. In the beginning, all businesses are created out of a need. A good or service is in demand by the consumer. From here, a business is started. The goods or services the company wants to provide are established and from there a business plan is created. For the sake of simplicity, the management/operations component is the one starting the business. From there, once the goods or services are identified and the business plan is in place, management must select a staff. And then, the preparation for the customer begins. Although the process may sound simple, everything the customer doesn't see involves hard labor and precision.

GOODS AND SERVICES

The goods sold or services rendered may seem like the easiest parts of a business, but it can be quite the opposite. In an example of a well-formed and organized business in the tourism industry, the goods or services from the business are the ignition point of the business. But the stage at which the target goods or services selected are blurred due to variables is when a business must decide whether to evolve or stay the same. For example, a restaurant may start out with a menu of a chosen cuisine it found by research was the most desirable to tourists in the area. But over time, the tastes and wants of the targeted tourists changed, causing a downward slope in sales. Does the business continue with its chosen cuisine because history shows that it is highly successful? Or does the team reassess the changing times and make changes to the menu gradually to gather more data around tourists' tastes? One would think the answer simple, that it should adjust its goods to best fit the current demand. But sometimes the amount of time, labor, and money that is required to make changes is not sufficient. Or sometimes the business is not willing to change for fear that it will lose its foundation customers, even though there is the opportunity to gain tenfold new customers.

The same is true of service-oriented businesses in the tourism industry. For instance, the hotel business. There are similar features of accommodations across the board such as a room, hotel concierge, and dining accessibility. A hotel business could provide five-star accommodations and customer service. But what if there were an increase of tourists requesting access to technology that the business does not have? More and more tourists are not unplugging while on holidays, and demand a business center or in-room technology that will allow them to connect with their work while on leisure travel trips. A business would then have to research to find out if its drop in reservations is in fact related to its lack of technology accessibility. It would also need to determine what it would look like to accommodate these guests and if not doing so would result in a consistently lower fill rate. As demonstrated, the goods and services initially chosen by a business can change over time, with many roadblocks in its way to evolving, some by choice and some by lack of resources. Either way, the choosing of a good or service by a business is not a guarantee of consistent demand.

MANAGEMENT/OPERATIONS

Management and operations are the ones in command of the show. They saw the need in the market, they chose their goods or services carefully, and they made a strategic plan. But then what? This is where the division between good management and bad management happens. One will often find in the tourism industry a clear difference between well-run businesses and the others. The management team of a well-run business is present at all times. They not only mold the business and choose its team, they show up, perform, and manage in a style that is flexible to change. There are many attributes that make up a successful manager in the tourism industry. Being able to manage his or her stress as well as that of the team with natural social skills honed by seasoned experience in his or her craft. The ability to multitask with the same ease as breathing, an innate passion for the business as well as a creative side that allows him or her to approach problems with multiple solutions. The bottom line is always the big picture focus for a qualified manager, so being able to make smart financial decisions is key.

A couple attributes of successful managers that are really effective behind the scenes are the ability to think systematically and the ability to recognize the way in which each individual team member communicates and learns best. These are the things that the tourist does not see for what they are. When a tourist acknowledges how smoothly a business is run while he or she is on holiday, he or she does not jump to the conclusion that the manager of operations must be a naturally highly skilled systematic thinker. Usually the tourist stops at the thought that things are running smoothly. But thinking systematically is not something that should be taken for granted, because a majority of the people don't do it. Systems thinking by definition is an all-inclusive method to analysis that concentrates on the way that a system's fundamental segments interconnect and how systems function over time and within the bigger picture of even larger systems. This type of thinking is an unarguable basic requirement for a successful manager. And one either naturally possesses it or doesn't.

Here is an example of how a manager instinctually thinks systematically. A restaurant is located at the center of a tourist destination. Imagine a manager walks into the establishment during a busy meal time. Immediately, he takes in the entire environment. During this assessment, which often takes place in seconds, he notes all of the red flags. To his left are two vacant tables that each seat up to six people. The tables are not bussed, but covered with dirty dishes as well as the bill left by the last guest. Off to his right is a group of impatient and confused people at the host stand, looking around because there is nobody there to greet them or provide them with information. With a far look into the kitchen area, the manager can see a haze of smoke, most likely caused by burning food, and notices the smell is starting to seep into the dining room.

The manager also notices that at one table of guests there is a man looking around for a staff member with an empty water glass in his hand.

So, what should the manager do first? An automatic first instinct would be to start clearing off the tables to his left in order to seat the customers. Or possibly run to the back of house to find staff to help the guests in the dining room or open a window in the kitchen. These are reasonable actions. But that's not what a business-minded, experience-building, systematic-thinking manager would do. In order to address all of the red flags in the quickest amount of time while maintaining a positive experience for all of the people involved, he would handle the situation differently.

After assessing all of the environment in less than ten seconds, the manager would wave to the guests at the host desk, noting he will be right with them. Then, the manager would pick up the water pitcher at the server station on his way over and fill the guest's empty glass, assuring him that his server will be right with him to check on him. While walking across the dining room towards the host desk, the manager would then quickly stop a busser and ask him to first go open a window in the kitchen, then return to the dirty tables to bus. By this time, he has arrived at the host station to greet the guests with cheer, take down their names, and let them know their table is being cleared now. Quickly, the manager would go to the back of the house to make sure any burning food has been disposed of and that the windows and back door were ajar. Next, the manager would find the appropriate staff and make sure they returned to their posts whether at the host stand, serving tables, or cleaning.

And why would the manager work this way? Because it systematically makes sense. The first concern is always the guest, so they were attended to first and assured they were recognized, easing their concern. Second, the manager's attention was quickly turned to the haze in the kitchen in order to prevent any hazardous environments before he finished addressing all of the immediate guest needs. The manager then personally double-checked the kitchen to assure there was no immediate cause for concern with the food, and that the proper ventilation was attended to. And finally, quickly placing the staff back to its proper positions, but not addressing any foul play in terms of incorrect placement of the team. A successful manager knows that he or she must first address the immediate needs of the experience by keeping everybody in their place, and talk with each staff member one on one to address any greater concerns with his or her performance at a later time. All in all, this entire scenario of red flags was successfully corrected in less than two minutes, systematically and with ease. This is how a manager should be acting and reacting every minute he or she is on a scene, whether in the front of the house or in back of the house. And this type of thinking and actions are what the tourist does not see. These constant, systematic responses to the environment are not what the guest sees. He or she sees only what the manager wants him or her to see, which is the most important aspect of running the show. Nobody wants the guest to see behind the scenes; it would only skew his or her perception of the business.

Another equally important manager attribute is being able to assess how a person best communicates and learns, and then readjusting one's own communication style to meet him or her where he or she needs to be met. In the above example, this would come in handy. The manager would know what staff members responded well to quick, immediate, and direct communication and which staff needed more explanation of immediate, expected actions. Not everybody learns the same way, and when managers choose a style and stick to it with all of their will, things inevitably don't work out. In order to reach a person, employee or customer, one must be able to assess within a brief interaction how that person best takes in information and responds. For example, some learn best with strict, bottom-line instructions, working at their peak in environments that demand results and provide strict guidelines. They are there to do what the manager expects, and have no problem following directions without question. Others could buckle immediately under these circumstances. These people react best to clear expectations explained at length, supported by a nurturing, open-door manager. This type of person may crave praise for his or her work every day in order to feel like a part of the team. Interacting with customers is the same game. Managers must be able to assess very quickly the way in which a customer needs to be treated. Some are fishing for over-the-top apologies for a mistaken food order, some customers want only an immediate correction of the mistake, and others look for an explanation of what went wrong. Every person is different and everyone learns differently; a manager must be able to read between the lines and alter his or her approach on the fly at all times with every interaction in order to maintain an ebb and flow that will allow him or her to continue running the business at its optimum pace. Again, the guests see polite, quick, and efficient staff providing them exceptional service. They do not see the effort and time that goes into it.

STAFF

Where would a business be without staff? They are the face of the tourism business, the first group of people with whom the tourist interacts. Although some strings are being pulled from behind the scenes, the staff are the impromptu actors. They are the team that is built to assist the business in upholding its mission and vision at all times. They were ideally and facelessly created by the business's strategic structure, then hand-picked by management to fill in the spots that were created for them. Successful managers know that the staff they choose is one of the, if not the most, important choices they can make. If just one staff member decides that he or she doesn't agree with the business's mission, or that he or she dislikes his or her job and the management team, this could become a quickly-moving poison flowing through all of the staff members, affecting their dedication and concentration. Without doubt, management must be able to sense such dissatisfaction and address it immediately. There is a reason behind the common expression that one bad apple can spoil a bunch. The same goes for staffing, and can come in many forms: one employee stealing money every shift, one employee being rude to customers on a daily basis, or one employee speaking disrespectfully about management when they work. Staffing is an important task that is not underestimated by successful managers.

The role of the staff member is unparalleled to any other component of the business structure. This is not to say other components are not as important, but the staff supply the human touch to a good or service. In a world dominated by technology and technological solutions to business problems, the human element can often be overlooked, underutilized, or taken for granted. Every business wants to create an ideal experience for the customer. But what components are constants and what components are variables? What factor can change the way the experience is flowing in a second's notice? A human. A staff member. What if during an experience the technology fails, causing a halt to the presentation created for the customer? Since the computer can't fix itself immediately, a staff member on site has the ability to step into the experience and recover the situation while the technological aspect is being recovered. Staff members provide immediate solutions, and can maintain and enhance the customer experience.

Managers strive to find always staff members that mirror them, and can make the same decisions they would make in their absence. But if a manager's expectations of his or her staff is high, he or she has an obligation to the business to provide a strict application and interview process as well as the necessary training to meet his or her expectations. And as most successful tourism business managers know, an employee must be equally as satisfied as the manager in order to create a connection to the business; they have to be willing and happy to provide the experience required by the business. Simple as that, right? Unfortunately, not so much. Let's break it down to a three-part process: hiring, training, and satisfaction.

How can a manager hire the right staff for his or her tourism business? What processes are set in place behind the scenes to choose first the staff to drive the experience? A manager is responsible for filling the positions that are outlined in the business plan. At this stage, he or she should have identified already the necessary positions to run the business with precise, detailed job descriptions. The manager should be screening first applicants for the basic requirements, then interviewing with a preferable two-person panel, arranging second interviews as well as hands-on trial sessions. The manager is not simply hiring a person based off of a paper or electronic resume or CV.

Once an applicant passes that step, he or she should be required to physically pass hands-on tasks that are provided by the manager and observed by a panel which could include managers, supervisors, and other staff already in place. Only at this time should a manager be ready to offer a position to an applicant. Unfortunately, this is not always how businesses play this out. Often, applicants are rushed through an interview and hired on the spot, usually due to a shortage in current staff and an immediate need to fill a position.

There is another aspect to the hiring responsibilities of the manager that is equally as important. Managers are also expected to be able to fire staff as systematically as they hire them, but a lot quicker. This is a big part of the behind-the-scenes portion of a tourism business that the tourist never sees, but it is a huge component to keeping the experience as flawless as possible. A common phrase in the industry, and one to undoubtedly follow, is "hire slowly and fire quickly." In other words, a business must follow an intense, thorough hiring practice in order to obtain the best staff for the job, but also be able to quickly identify the bad apples and, without hesitation, address the situation. Some situations allow for the options to retrain employees, reassess the way they learn in order to help them better fill positions, or connect with them and address and correct unwanted behavior. But sometimes the options are not as desirable as these. Sometimes a manager must be able to separate business from personal feelings and fire the employee who is clearly not able to fulfill the job tasks, no matter what level of training he or she has been offered. There are also the very common scenario of a staff member who is not doing his or her job as assigned by choice and therefore not carrying out the optimum customer experience as the business has outlined in its training expectations. A manager must be able to extinguish fires, which includes often the dismissal of staff who are not in line with the company mission for one reason or another.

Businesses are responsible for training their staff to levels that let them take full responsibility for meeting expectations of their positions. Managers should have well-formed training manuals in order to provide all expectations, and the steps required of them. The manual should be used in conjunction with all training sessions and as a reference for employees, when needed. Basically, if a manager has a particular expectation of an employee in terms of performance, then the manager is expected by the business to explain the expectation in detail and provide ample training until both the manager and staff member are satisfied and confident in performing the tasks at hand. But that is not always how it happens. Businesses in a fast-paced industry that are constantly in need of more help tend to rush their hiring and training procedures in order to get staff into position quicker. This puts the staff members, by no fault of their own, in sink-or-swim situations. Some employees flourish and are motivated by a challenge to figure things out on their own, while most others become lost if there are no boundaries or clear expectations, which sets them up for automatic failure.

Satisfaction. This word comes up all over the map in the tourism industry. It starts with the tourist's satisfaction with his or her travels and the businesses he or she encountered. A manager's satisfaction with his or her staff is equally important. But what about the employee's satisfaction with his or her employer? This is one of those areas that divides the mediocre businesses from the extraordinary businesses. Not all managers consider the satisfaction level of the staff to be of importance. Often, the traditional expectation is in place that they are there to serve the business and are compensated financially in return. Employee satisfaction comes in that next level of craving to satisfy the customer, those leaps and bounds taken in order to provide a life-altering experience for every customer. Successful businesses that take this into consideration are in that top layer of businesses reaching beyond the norm in order to serve. They realize that a happy employee equals a genuine and relentless presentation of circumstances in order to provide an unwaveringly positive, memorable experience for the customer. Without the buying in of all parties involved in creating the customer experience, the experience will not meet the standards set forth before it. The happiness and satisfaction with the business on a whole directly affects the experience of each and every tourist.

Once hired and trained and raring to go, staff members should be experts at hiding the web of intricate systems and processes demanding a consistent performance in order to maintain the stage set for the customer. Their role is to seamlessly walk back and forth from backstage to the main stage protecting the internal design in order to provide a positive sensory experience for the customer at all times. The idea is to never let the tourist know what is going on behind the curtain. Witnessing the organized chaos behind the scenes could end in an immediate disconnect for the customer from his or her leisure holiday. The idea is to create a perception that everything is running smoothly when really, as those in the tourism industry already know, this is not the case. That doesn't mean that the goal of the business is not being met. Organized chaos is a situation in which there seems to be a lot of confusion and no organization, but desired results are still yielded. This term singlehandedly sums up the behind-the-scenes tourism business.

But with staffing come the problems that have always plagued the tourism and hospitality industry and sometimes there are only the "best" options to solve them, which still may not be the best scenarios for the business. For instance, a shortage in staff. No matter the efforts a business takes, especially in tourism, the industry is cursed with the reoccurring problem of staff shortage. This problem can come up unexpectedly when staff decide to quit with no notice, call in sick, stop showing up for work, or are asked to leave immediately by management due to serious offenses. But it really bubbles up much deeper inside the infrastructure. The real problem facing the tourism industry today regarding staff shortages stems from the problems with staff recruitment and training mentioned above. Again, when there is not a clear and organized foundation set down from the beginning, problems are guaranteed to arise.

Successful managers start with sound practices like careful and calculated recruitment, proper training, and staff appreciation systems set up to keep employees satisfied, all of which lower the percentage of staff shortages and empower their businesses to be able to make decisions quickly due to their preparation. It cannot be stressed enough: preparation!

GUESTS AND CUSTOMERS

Without the customer, there is no demand. Without demand, there is no tourism industry. So from the get-go, it is clear how important the customer is. There is a reason why they say the customers are always right. It's because they are. Whatever feelings they have and whatever actions they take are warranted simply because they exist. If a customer is angry about a service not performed up to his or her expectations, the situation is real and must be addressed accordingly. If a customer feels he or she was treated with disrespect, what he or she feels is real, and needs to be addressed immediately. Basically, if they feel it, it's real. So no matter what a business, manager, or staff member thinks is true, they must always respect the feelings and perceptions of the customer in order to maintain a positive, seamless experience.

A difference in the way a consumer is perceived by staff members in the tourism industry begins with a simple term. A *customer* is simply a person or organization that buys goods or services from a store or business. A *guest* is a person who is invited in to take part in an event or function organized by another person, as a special honor, or to receive the hospitality of another. As you can see, the difference between the two words is clear. So, if you owned a business, how would you want to relate to and have your staff relate to the people who want your goods or services? Why do hotels have *guests* while supermarkets have *customers*? Is there a difference between the people who want accommodation services and those who want to buy food? In order for the current generation to get the most out of the market in their business, it is necessary that they start by acknowledging their consumers as they would want their entire staff to relate to them. And in the tourism industry, businesses must lay the foundation behind the scenes by not only referring to the consumers of their goods and services as guests, but by creating experiences that honor all of their guests from beginning to end, seamlessly providing unforgettable, positive sensory experiences. Again, easier said than done? You bet.

Some of the top companies in the world have adopted this terminology in order to view their consumers in a way that sets the stage for an experience instead of a purchase. By setting the expectation to staff members that they are there to cater to a guest, not just a consumer, it immediately creates a perception of service and hospitality. At this point, the business is not there simply to provide a good or service or to explain their offerings in hopes that a consumer makes a purchase. But with one word, they are setting the expectation that no matter what, their consumers, their guests, are there to be appreciated, catered to, acknowledged, and respected regardless of their intent to purchase a good or service. This doesn't mean the company does not have a bottom line on which to focus. But in turn, by creating this welcoming environment flawlessly with every guest, the company creates a branded experience that will grow beyond each person who visits that establishment. Again, why wouldn't we warmly welcome the people who mean so much to us?

SETTING THE STAGE

There are many businesses in the tourism industry, but the main stage-setters of a destination are a few key players whom every tourist will encounter maintaining the stage at all times. Imagine whom the tourist will encounter from the second he or she steps onto the plane (or train, bus, or boat) to the destination. These are the big guns who work 24/7, acting a part in order for the tourist to enjoy his or her experience. Picture you have planned an adventurous holiday to escape from daily life. You would expect that from the second you walk out of your door with your luggage to the second you walk back into your home that you are on a leisure holiday. In order for this experience to take form, all of the businesses in the tourism industry must be participating in that experience, and maintaining that stage at all times. There is no down time or break for the businesses participating in the tourist's journey. These businesses are on stage, maintaining an act, while the wheels turn behind the scenes. But if this is the case, the optimal agenda of the tourism businesses, why is it that not all holidays are as picturesque as one would imagine?

Unfortunately, not every tourism business is in the same game as the others. As previously mentioned, sometimes businesses focus too harshly on the bottom line and miss the entire experience in the arena. Others are working with consumers while their competition is serving guests. And some have no idea what it is exactly they are supposed to be doing in the first place. This happens because there are so many individual businesses within the larger scope of the industry; for example, transportation. An airport is a business. It has managers, staff, customers, and a large amount of goods and services to offer. An airport can follow all of the rules of etiquette, treating its consumers as guests, going out of its way to maintain a sensory experience, and providing a pleasant waiting area for the tourist's next step. But just because the airport is everything the tourist could imagine in his or her vivid adventure does not mean that every single airline in that airport is playing the same game. Unfortunately, each airline is a separate business playing by different rules. Once the tourist steps into the gate area of that airline, the entire scene could change. Some maintain the experience set up by the airport or exceed its set expectation. But often they don't.

The airline industry is one of the few players in the tourism industry that has not caught fire as quickly with the same concepts as others. But the airline industry has made major changes over the years to keep up with now commonplace international travel that was once only for a set level of individuals. Airlines have been able to lower prices, offer more flights, provide discounts, and reward travel, all to keep up with competition. But there is only so much airlines are able to do, and willing to do, in the air that would make a difference in the tourists' decision. When booking travel, most people look for the cheapest airline in order to compensate for the funds they will need at their destinations. Airlines know this. They are good at the discount game, but what is pushing them to provide an onboard experience that is different from the rest? Some airlines have luxury accommodations, but these are often amenities that only the wealthy can afford. In terms of creating an experience that is desirable and even anticipated, the airline industry is lacking. It may be because it is aware that in order to get certain places, tourists don't have another choice except to fly. Why would it go out of its way to enhance the experience? Or is it because they feel there is not much they can provide at that height, in those quarters, that would make a difference to the experience? Only the airlines know the reason. But one would think that business common sense would lead them to strive at excelling in customer service, reaching above and beyond to make an uncomfortable situation more enjoyable, and taking on the challenge to reach more tourists and consumers. There are exceptions to this overall perception of the airline industry, though. These airlines have been able to make not only the best of a cramped experience, but create an experience to which tourists look forward. By attending to all the tourist's sensory needs, these airlines have exceeded all expectations. Not only have they reached the tourist aesthetically, but personally. By putting guests at ease with friendly conversation and lightly comedic airline safety and information videos, the airlines are able to set the stage for a less stressful flight than expected. By adding in extra perks during the flight such as free drinks, snacks, movies, pillows, and blankets, they put the guest at ease physically. And continued attention and conversation from flight attendants keep the tourists as comfortable and stress-free as possible. There is not a lot of behind-the-scenes area on an airplane. But by maintaining the stage throughout the experience consistently, the airline industry is able to accommodate guests with a thorough welcoming experience.

The other businesses in the sector are expected to maintain equally the stage throughout the tourist's experience. There is nothing more deflating for a tourist than experiencing an environment that is all but welcoming during his or her journey. For example, a constant behind-the-scenes view can be not only disturbing to a tourist's experience, but stressful and depressing. Imagine being on a business trip and having a wonderful experience flying into your destination on an airline that exceeded all expectations. Your taxi ride to the hotel is seamless, bringing you to the front door of your hotel. Then you step inside and the mirage has vanished. None of the staff acknowledges your arrival into the hotel. Within your ten-second assessment of the environment, you witness staff sitting down in the lobby's guest area and a door open from the front desk area into the back of house through which you see and hear management arguing with a staff member. You begin waiting in line behind thirteen other people to check in while holding all of your luggage. Before you check in, you reassess your options, wondering if it would be worse to get on your phone to cancel your reservation and book another hotel in your foreign destination. Unfortunately, some businesses are not able to seamlessly divide their behind-the-scenes environment with the experience meant for the guest.

Entertainment, attractions, and restaurants are also part of the full experience for the tourist. Luckily, businesses whose main focus is on entertainment and themed experiences often have an upper hand at delivering to and exceeding expectations of the tourist. There are even tourist attractions that combine entertainment with attractions and restaurants. These venues are dinner theatres. What some in the business say is the next level to dining and entertainment, and the progression of the ultimate tourist attraction, are dining establishments that truly define the experience destination. Places like Heart in Ibiza, Spain; Igor's in Singapore; and Teatro Zinzanni in San Francisco, California have set the bar for themed experiences that cross food with entertainment. These types of venues create consistent themed experiences from the outside of the restaurant through a guest's exit after the show. Every employee, from the cooks to the servers and the hosts to the stage actors, plays a part in an elaborate story. The experiences engages all of the guests, intertwining them in the story as the evening progresses. These establishments aim to transform dinner theatres into intriguing sensory experiences that leave the guests wanting more. With experiences that never falter and the illusion that there is no backstage, these types of attractions create an intimate connection with every guest that leaves lasting impressions far beyond the guest's time spent within the environment.

CULTURAL ISSUES AND STEREOTYPES

The tourism industry, with all of its dramatically increasing success in the global economy, still continues to struggle with image and reputation when it comes to its workforce. The industry is often stereotyped as low paying with no career advancement possibilities. The sector is thought to recruit heavily from young and migrant workers (those working outside of their home country), and provide inadequate internal training for those lacking soft skills. Due to the stereotypes of the industry itself, its workforce has been steadily looked down upon globally as a lower class of people. Cultural issues also play a part in the negative view of the tourism industry. When a large part of the tourism industry workforce is made up of workers from other countries, there are automatic labels and perceptions of the industry and businesses. But are these stereotypes of the industry true? And does that automatically make these facts negative? Let's take a closer look.

Globalization has changed the travel and tourism industry immeasurably. It is the process in which businesses, technologies, and philosophies spread throughout the world, and it has made the global economy an interconnected marketplace without boundaries of country or continent. It has facilitated change and growth in the industry and an increased need for more workers. And with constant demand growing, often supply is hastily acquired to fill this need. This is where the quick hiring of massive amounts of people happens, often involving lower-paid workers. It is a fact that migrant workers tend to settle for work that has a lower pay rate. They are not native to the country in which they seek work, automatically lowering their expertise of the destination and specific work skills necessary to work there. Therefore, it is challenging to gain employment in other sectors, but the tourism industry, specifically hospitality, is known for its heavy need for large amounts of people and easy job access for foreigners settling down in new areas and traveling through. Moving to another country is difficult for anybody. It is no surprise that if a foreigner moves to a new country, it is usually a better location for him or her for one reason or another. To gain any employment at that time can be a positive situation. To dig even deeper, a tourism business's number one expense is labor. And when a business is looking to lower its expenses, it looks often to its highest expense. And in order to lower the labor expense, a business tends to hire staff willing to accept lower pay.

Every country is different in the way it views foreign workers. In some countries, they are referred to as *expatriates*, in other nations as *foreigners*, and in some as simply *migrants*. By being part of the tourism industry and paid lower wages, these workers are generally looked down upon, as are almost all workers in what is referred to globally as the lower classes. To challenge this stereotype, most people don't see what foreign workers bring to the tourism industry. They bring to a business new skills, innovations, and knowledge that they gained either in their home countries or while traveling through other nations. Having a global perspective in the tourism industry brings a positive contribution to the business. And for a business that is working on an upper hand in the industry, having a workforce that brings a multicultural face to the business often makes tourists feel more welcome when interacting not only with the host community, but with possible familiar nationalities from their regions as well. The tourism industry is an international business, so why wouldn't a diverse cultural staff be desirable? The businesses in this case are getting a win-win when they hire a diverse staff at a lower rate. Some businesses are putting their business at an advantage with such a diverse staff without even knowing it, but in the end the workforce is still being financially underappreciated, which does in fact keep them separated from other, higher, classes.

As if being perceived as lower class due to income wasn't enough, workers in the tourism and hospitality industry are perceived as lower individuals overall.Although working in the service industry may be ideal to some who enjoy it and excel in it, a majority of the world does not see it as a glamorous job. But what percentage of people do have glamorous jobs? Although the answer is not many, jobs in tourism and hospitality are knocked down even further as the closest jobs to the distant servant class as one can get in contemporary times. Service work is demanding and undervalued. And unfortunately, the legislation protecting this workforce in most countries is not enforced.

One of the most frustrating things for an employee in the service industry is the knowledge that he or she is being paid a lower wage while a majority of the population in higher classes could not perform his or her job at even an entry level. Those in the tourism industry know that their work is not only physically challenging, but psychologically challenging as well. Just as a specialist in finances for Fortune 500 companies has skills not easily acquired, so does the specialized workforce of the hospitality and tourism industry. Not anybody can jump into the shoes of the big-time accountant, but neither would he or she be able to walk in the shoes of a hospitality worker in his or her tenth hour on his or her feet serving guests and juggling unknown variables. But it is not just the entry-level, lower-paid employees of the industry that get stereotyped negatively. Even those at the very top of the chain managing multiple venues within a company of hotels and restaurants are put into the same category. Even though they are at a management level, due to the industry in which they work, they are not viewed as equals to managers in other sectors. These top professionals in the industry, often having acquired undergraduate and graduate degrees in hospitality, business, and management, are still lumped together with the stereotype of the industry. Although not all countries hold this perspective, unfortunately, many do. With travel and tourism taking over the number-one economic sector globally, what will it take to change the perception, value, and pay rate of its workforce?

Locals of a destination in some nations often shy away from employment in the tourism industry. The perception of the sector is that it provides lower pay and has lower skill requirements. Often countries have a misperception of the industry that all of the jobs in it are for tour guiding and hospitality serving. Also, many cultures do not encourage participation in the sector as it is not a familiar part of their values. All of these misconceptions about the industry rise from a lack of education about the travel and tourism business. In many nations the sector is not highlighted as one with opportunities, and there is never any mention of higher education in the sector. But in reality, the travel and tourism industry has a huge impact on the global economy, and often tourism and hospitality management begins with a business education. Not only are schools not educating students about the career opportunities in the industry, but the overall view of the industry is incorrect in many places. If you walk into a book store and ask to see the tourism section, it does not exist. Rather, you will be ushered to a section full of guide books and maps in the travel area. In order for the conditions within the tourism industry to improve, the picture painted of the industry from the outside must change.

THE VARIABLES

But no matter how much planning, organizing, and preparing is done behind the scenes, no business can predict all of the variables that will come its way on a day-to-day basis. Variables around a problem that are not under the control of the problem solver occur. In other words, variables are problems that pop up which may be solved but are not under the manager's control. Common uncontrollable variables in the tourism industry typically involve staffing, customers, economy, natural disasters, weather, and technology. Knowing one's business and having seasoned management can help prepare for when these variables attack. When a natural disaster or extreme weather hits, a business that is prepared in terms of safety for the staff and building will be better prepared to cater to its guests during these types of situations. The phrase "Please put on your air masks before assisting others" is metaphorically applicable to any situation that requires a person or group of people to assist others. As for the economy, there is only so much a business can do to prepare for ups and downs in the industry and the destination's economy. The best solution for this problem is for the business to be aware and educated about what is going on in the economy so it might make the most appropriate financial decisions that will cause the least negative effect on the business.

Another behind-the-scenes variable that managers have to juggle is technology. In hopes of always keeping technological problems offstage so as to not disrupt a guest's experience, businesses prepare themselves for a list of general technology problems that arise. Although technological advances are surpassing expectations daily, more and more problems come along with that advancement. And while those problems are in the troubleshooting stage, consumers of technology are forced to remain patient for solutions. But when problems arise that need immediate solutions, businesses and managers must be able to address them with the best possible solution that aids at that time in maintaining the desired guest experience. Although most people, including tourists, are aware that technology is not perfect and that errors do occur, that's the last excuse they want to hear on their ten-day luxury holiday or important business trip.

The variables connected to staffing and customers are human elements of the industry. No matter how much screening or training is done for an employee, there is no guarantee that a person will act, or react, as assumed. People are complex, thinking, and feeling variables. The only preparation to counteract the unexpected actions of a staff member or guest is previous experience. With the combined previous experiences of a large amount of people, including staff and guests, the odds are better that somebody is familiar with a scenario that pops up unexpectedly and is able to lend his or her expertise to the solution. And just as people are complex, so is the tourism industry behind the scenes.

Part Five

Theme Parks and Tourism

The theme park is an experience that intimately belongs to the tourism industry. Not only is it all-encompassing of the goal to create a fluid, sensory experience for the guest, but the theme park is the original creation of the experience industry. That's not to say that hotels, airlines, and tourist destination restaurants did not exist before the theme park. But the creation of theme parks heavily influenced the sector becoming up to par where it is today with other sectors in the world economy. Theme parks are now one of the biggest motivators for tourists choosing a destination. With more and more theme parks being built all over the world, the more competition there is in enticing tourists. And with tourists attending theme parks in greater numbers, their expectations becoming more sophisticated, parallel to advances in technology and innovations. Instead of just growing in terms of numbers, the theme park industry is bursting is every direction, evolving at a rapid pace. It is one of the few pieces of the tourism industry that has changed consistently with advances in technology. While other businesses tend to fight advancement, sticking to more traditional values and roles, the theme park industry has thrived on what is new and better, with individual parks constantly battling each other over who will lead the way with newer and better innovations. The theme park is starting to take control of the tourism industry, leading it into the future, pulling it out of the pack, and helping it to stay as one of the top economic sectors in the world.

Theme parks have also sparked a new trend in the tourism industry with their newly formed niche of tourists motivated by theme park travel. These tourists are motivated by thrill seeking. Not only do they focus on adventure traveling, but specifically travel to theme parks across the globe. Supported by websites and organizations, this niche of tourists is rapidly increasing in number. So long as the theme park industry thrives and exceeds expectations in innovation, this special group of tourists will flourish, appreciating the experiences created by these destinations and pushing the industry with higher expectations. It is a positive relationship of supply and demand so unique, it is set apart from other sections in the tourism industry.

Unlike other sections of the industry, theme parks, on a global scale, tend to have no limitations of seasons or off-peak times due to their strategic locations. Rarely will you see a theme park in a location that is controlled by weather. And those that are affected by undesirable weather are prepared with many sections of their parks unaffected by adverse conditions that are able to carry on with business at all times of the year. Theme parks' attendance has continued to increase at an unstoppable rate from year to year in all areas of the world. The large numbers that theme parks are able to pull in are unparalleled to any other tourist attraction. And although the tourism sector is recognizing the success the theme park industry has to offer, the sector itself continues to diversify its assets, not putting all of its eggs in one basket. In other words, in order to succeed, the sector must continue to balance its dependencies, investing and supporting all moving parts in order to maintain checks and balances for the greater good of the sector.

The only problem the theme park industry has had in terms of recognition is the definition for the public of what a theme park really is. Although there is not always a correct distinction between an amusement park and a theme park, the two are very separate things. The basic formula for a theme park, invented by Walt Disney, is that rides and attractions are interwoven with a story that carries through the entire park. By incorporating whimsical landscapes, music, characters, and other sensory elements, theme parks have guests that become automatic active participants in the story instead of passive passengers. Storytelling, lighting, composition, and multi-dimensional spaces all enhance the guest's experience and help maintain the story seamlessly from the entrance to the exit of the park. When theme parks first began with Walt Disney, it was the first time that landscapes and costumes were used outside of the motion picture business. The set of a movie became a relevant environment for theme parks, utilizing many talented specialists.

Amusement parks, on the other hand, forgo storytelling for the most part. Instead, these parks are filled with individual rides and attractions that don't necessarily connect to one another in theme. The rides often offer thrills simply for the thrills' sakes, not to contribute to the guest's visit on a whole. Amusement parks no doubt offer amusement on many levels, but have stories or themes that do not interact from one attraction or ride to another. The staff at amusement parks do not play a part in a story or support an overall experience for the guest. Although amusement parks were the only type of park in the past and still exist today, and the theme park is thriving, most parks now fall in a gray area. These parks strive to be more than roller coaster scream zones, but lack the commitment to tell cohesive stories. So while there are many entertaining, exciting, and thrilling parks all over the world, theme parks are what is catapulting art, technology, and innovation into the future.

HISTORY OF THE THEME PARK

The theme park has been around for centuries, evolving from the earliest times and building on markets, exhibitions, and fairs of the past. Variations of all kinds have been progressing from one to another, pushing the envelope further and further as time and technology evolved. Fairs were any gathering of people for a variety of entertainment or activities and were temporary, lasting a scheduled amount of time from an afternoon to weeks. One of the first known was the periodic fair of the Middle Ages, traced back to the early twelfth century. These fairs developed as temporary markets important for long-distance and international trade. During this time, most fairs were tied to a Christian religious occasion and only held in larger organized cities where authorities could overlook them. Often, people who did not practice Christianity did not attend these fairs out of concern that they might not interact well with the culture or beliefs. The fairs evolved and some became pleasure gardens, such as the famed Vauxhall Gardens in London where people went to escape the hustle, bustle, and grime of the city. Lasting through the seventeenth, eighteenth, and nineteenth centuries, the Gardens offered acres of trees, flowers, and trails. Paintings, sculptures, and musical performances were also enjoyed within the Garden. And although originally a place of high culture and refinement, the Garden later became a favorite place for dancing and other mainstream entertainment.

Soon the fairs evolved into mass gatherings of people for entertainment purposes at which the public could *interact* with the show. The notorious freak shows were common attractions at these fairs, bending the illusion of reality with presentations of people and oddities that had never been seen. Often these people were gathered literally from locations around the world and brought back to these fairs to be displayed as what locals would consider odd presentations. Fairs of this time also introduced mechanical and steam-powered rides, opening the era of the fun fair ride. These rides were initially precarious in construction, offering a true scare when ridden. Soon after came the full concept of a fixed park for amusement, which was developed through the world's fairs global exhibitions, first taking place in 1851 in London, England. These fairs were pivotal in the advancement of the industry. And as time moved on, the idea of fairs continued to be molded by innovations of the times.

The events spread globally, incorporating new ideas with cultural traditions, spawning subcategories of fairs and amusement parks. The first permanently enclosed entertainment area owned by one company was Coney Island in 1895. Its short-lived Dreamland was one of the most ambitious amusement parks ever constructed. Lit by one million electric bulbs, attractions included a refrigerated ride through the mountains of Switzerland, a gondola ride through the canals of Venice, and a relaxing time at a Japanese Tea House. The park was also scattered with freak shows and strange exhibits, including one where visitors could observe premature babies being kept alive by incubators. Although this would be a quite horrible and unethical "attraction" at a fair today, incubators were a completely new and highly untested technology at that time. They served as an exhibition because they were thought to be a way of the future most interesting to people. Oftentimes, exhibitions that give us a peek into the future are the most treasured, and most visited, exhibitions at any event worldwide. A promise, if you will, of the future.

The amusement park began popping up in major cities, attracting those with newly disposable income, until the industry first declined in the 1930s, when the global economy took a hit. During this time, there was no demand and no supply. Entertainment became something only the very wealthy, or those in political power, pursued for enjoyment. But as the years went by, there was a surge of need for entertainment. It was no longer just for disposable incomes, but a need to celebrate life after wartime. This helped the entertainment industry take off again. And in this rebound, the theme park industry, and the world, changed with the emergence of the magical Walt Disney. Not only did he change the landscape and playing field of the amusement park industry, but he was the inventor of the theme park.

But Walt Disney's path started well before the opening of his first theme park in 1955. Mr. Disney had been a cultural icon long before the gates opened up to Disneyland in Anaheim, California. Walt Disney, by trade an entrepreneur, was a well-established animator. Born in 1901 in Chicago, Illinois, Disney eventually found his way to Hollywood, California to further pursue his interest in animation, where he and his brother opened Disney Brothers' Studios. It wasn't long until Mickey, Donald, Goofy, and Pluto showed up, followed by the full-length film *Snow White and the Seven Dwarfs* in 1937. After the success of the first animated feature in America made in Technicolor, the Walt Disney Studios opened in 1939 in Burbank, California. While the studio took off in feature animation films, World War II erupted. Disney was lassoed into a partnership with the military, providing training and instruction films as well as bringing humor to military units to boost morale; his company took a back seat. The animation business started up again with the end of the war in the late 1940s, which is when Disney began sketches for the park. The ideas further developed after his trip to Children's Fairyland in Oakland, California, about a six-hour drive north of his studios. The park had opened its doors in 1950, built as a land of storybook adventures on the shores of Lake Merritt. It was truly one of the first children's theme parks. Filled with storybook attractions, live animals, and entertainment, fairytale landscapes had costumed guides to lead children. Walt Disney was so taken aback by the small children's theme park, he was motivated to build a larger version, and did just that. Five years later, he opened the doors to Disneyland. On July 17, 1955, Walt Disney dedicated his park as a happy place, a source of joy and inspiration to the world. Not forgetting what he experienced at Children's Fairyland, Disney hired both their first executive director as well as one of their puppeteers to join him at his company.

But Walt Disney did more than open an amusement park with rides and characters. He actually changed the world. He altered how people perceived entertainment and how they experienced…an experience. He creatively developed the very first full theme park. What differentiated his design from those of the past was his approach to the overall experience. He focused on the bigger picture, and created a living cartoon world that immersed guests in the rides and attractions not only to entertain but to involve them in the story that was carried throughout the park. He was able to incorporate and orchestrate a stage over the entire experience. In order to successfully direct the show, Disney referred to his employees as cast members. These cast members were in costume and character at all times while within the park, and responsible for maintaining the production of tastes, sounds, sights, smells, and textures, all that helped create a unique sensory experience. Still to this day, if you walk into any Disney park across the globe, you will notice that you never see a cast member out of character, and can always expect a return smile from any member of the Disney team when you look his or her way. And to further involve the clientele of the park, Walt Disney referred to them automatically as guests, never customers. This idea has carried on through the years, and through many different businesses in the industry. A quick way to assess how a business is set up in the tourism industry is to see in its handbook how it refers to its clientele, either as customers or guests. This simple gesture can determine how a business views one of its most valuable assets, as one who makes a purchase or as one who is there to partake in an experience set forth by the company.

Because Disney set the stage with high expectations from day one, Disneyland and all of Disney's parks continue to maintain the same unique, seamless experience throughout every establishment by every cast member at every location. By creating such an innovative way to interact with people, both guests and cast members alike, he was able to build an empire that continues to flourish and never falters. And in the bigger picture, Disney pioneered the experience economy through his parks, adding a layer of value that did not previously exist in the minds of business owners in the industry. His business model at that time was so far ahead of the minds of many people that other businesses in the industry took years to catch up to his innovative way of thinking and his almost magical way of creating a never-before-seen experience. To this day, sadly, there are still businesses that have not caught up to his way of thinking. Those are the many, many businesses that have either failed or are on their way down a path of no return, and no-return customers as well.

IMAGINEERING: INNOVATIONS AND TECHNOLOGY CHANGING REALITY

Walt Disney invented more than just the modern theme park. His contributions gave birth to the experience industry, providing a springboard for other theme parks in the Disney empire and all other theme park companies. There is also a term that stands out when people think of Disney: *Imagineering*. The term is a portmanteau, a combination of the words *imagination* and *engineer*. Although this is a word intimately connected to Disney, it was coined before this connection; it was used by an American aluminum company in many ads as well as mentioned in other published works in the 1940s and 1950s. Disney used the word first in 1952 and applied for a trademark in 1967. Walt Disney Imagineering (WDI, or simply Imagineering) is the design and development arm of the Walt Disney Company and is responsible for the creation and construction of all Disney theme parks, resorts, cruise ships, and other entertainment venues.

The Walt Disney Company, then and today, refers to all of its illustrators, architects, engineers, lighting designers, graphic designers, show writers, and other talented team members as Imagineers. Although their headquarters are in Glendale, California, the roles of these Imagineers extends far beyond the office to spending long periods of time on location at the many Disney parks across the world in order to maintain an intimate relationship with their work. What truly differentiates Disney's methods from the manner in which most companies are run is its Imagineering expectations and principles. Fully embracing and expressing originality, Disney Imagineers are steered by a few guiding principles when creating new attractions and improving existing ones. First, they are guided by the "blue sky speculation" principle. This encourages them to generate ideas that have no limitations and are beyond belief at their time of inception. Walt Disney created an environment that still holds strong today; Imagineers start their creative processes with the wildest, boldest, and most detailed ideas they can come up with. He felt that pushing his team members to operate under the notion that if they dreamt it, they could built it would set their adventures apart from those of all other companies. And he was right.

Walt Disney also followed a principle that if every business would attempt just to follow, it would be better. In opposition to most businesses who stick to an "if it ain't broke, don't fix it" mentality, Disney took the stance that there is always room for innovation and improvement. He believed that as long as there was imagination in the world, Disney parks would never be complete and that principle holds true today. There is not one original Disney attraction that has not been updated or reinvented over the years by the Imagineers. They took to heart his vision and passed it on through generations who are passing it down today to future creators.

This forward thinking of Disney in terms of always enhancing and improving upon what is already there has influenced some of the most successful businesses in the world. His game plan at that time was innovative, unique, unheard of, and lofty. Sadly, even with the working, living examples of his principles present in the world like an open book, businesses are not all copying his model of success today. Businesses tend to fall into a rut and become afraid to inherit any ideas or principles that are not mainstream, traditional, or equations for what they see as success. These are the businesses that are far from being in touch with their guests' experiences, focusing on the bottom line instead. But imagine every tourism business taking on the principles of Disney. Competition in the marketplace would become fierce, and businesses would push up against one another to spawn more and more creative ideas to enhance the guests' experiences. Imagine an entire industry not afraid to break boundaries, and working with no limitations. Disney laid out a very clear, simple, and successful plan for his company for all to see. What was once clean cut, clear, and creative is still so in the World of Disney. It's almost a mystery why a business in the same industry wouldn't adopt his principles, which have proven successful decade after decade. Perhaps these principles are just too far out of the box for them. But with the rapid growth of innovation and technology, it is becoming a must to jump on board and embrace the future. Disney happened to do it first.

The Walt Disney Imagineering crew members have been granted more than 115 patents over the years for interactive technology, special effects, and ride systems. They have been noted as the front-runners of technological advances not only in their industry, but across many platforms of entertainment. They are known specifically and most famously for their unique development of Audio-Animatronics that brought 3D characters to life for the first time. The Enchanted Tiki Room in Disneyland was the first attraction to use this technology, followed by the 1964 World's Fair that featured an Audio-Animatronics figure of Abraham Lincoln that awed its onlookers. Today, this technology is used throughout Disney parks, and has also inspired the creation of an Autonomatronic figure that would be capable of sensing, seeing, hearing, and responding to a person in conversation. Although distinct from the Audio-Animatronic figures programmed by Disney with speech and sounds, the advanced close form of this invention would be considered artificial intelligence, an android-type robot. This type of "character" is quite possibly the future of cast members throughout the entertainment industry. One wonders if Disney knew to what he was paving the road, and how he would react to its use and success today.

The hallmarks of a Disney experience include a very specific mood that is set intentionally and delicately. The story a Disney theme park tells is similar to the experience of entering a show. Without prompting, one would know unmistakably when one has entered a Disney theme park.Every detail is calculated and thoughtfully engineered, from the smell of cotton candy on Main Street to the unique sound of each separate land and adventure in the park. Disney parks invented, and have perfected, the art of the show. Disney *is* innovations and technology that are changing reality. But where is everybody else in the tourism industry? Maybe not every business can be exactly like Disney. But all businesses can, if they are willing to, adapt to the increase of technology with innovative and forward thinking. Both technology and innovation are central to improving businesses and destination competitiveness in the industry as well as to improving directly the tourist's experience. The tourism industry has a unique opportunity. It is a sector that has overcome many barriersto global travel by embracing technological advances. The world's economic advancement is neatly tied to technology, but the tourism sector in particular can consistently utilize technology and innovation to gain an upper hand in the global economy.

Tourism, like the world, is constantly being shaped by technology. Travel is full of opportunities that can positively frame the guest experience. Now that tourists search the Internet for ideas about traveling before even researching destinations, businesses in the tourism sector have every opportunity to seize this advancement in technology and create new ways to reach the tourist and keep him or her involved. Disney simply pioneered the idea of reaching guests through creative avenues, grabbing their attention and pulling them into a full experience. It is now up to the tourism industry to keep up with the call to change the future by coming up with innovative ideas, continuing to evolve, and not fighting against the current of time. Businesses must realize that they cannot only use technology to guide tourists to their destinations but to create an environment with which they can interact once they arrive. Most importantly, these tourism businesses must realize, as Walt Disney did, that the experience phase does not end once the guests left the arena. Their experiences will influence others to dream and be inspired to travel to their destinations. The cycle of travel continues every time a person travels. It is up to the businesses to engage with those travelers with an open mind in order to continually improve upon their experiences.

A GLOBAL LOOK AT THE THEME PARK INDUSTRY TODAY

In a field that is constantly evolvinglike the theme park industry, it is hard to keep up with the saturated market of businesses joining the game. There are clearly industry leaders, specifically the Walt Disney Company, that continue to lead the world in unstoppable innovation. But other companies are starting to catch up as more and more people join the ranks of "Imagineers" across the globe. The competition has increased, as has the demand from guests overwhelmed by the growing market for unique, out-of-this-world experiences. With all of this happening on a global scale, governing bodies and organizations are vital to contain the organized chaos of such a creative field.

There are many global organizations that do just that for the industry. It often takes global connections and specialists to bring together all of the creators, developers, designers, and producers in the industry. These organizations bring together those who create successful, engaging attractions and experiences in the travel and tourism sector, including theme parks. The Themed Entertainment Association (TEA) is one of those organizations whose members are considered innovators in their field. They bring about one-of-a-kind projects and bring new levels to guest engagement. Their goal is to focus on the guest experience and the vital niche of the culture that is motivated by experience. Organizations like TEA provide a networking platform for creative companies, suppliers, technical specialists, and owners. They connect businesses with the experts they need to continue advancing their businesses through technology and innovation. They are a key player that is growing bigger every year in the theme park industry, reaching more destinations and creating more relationships in this future-forward business.

Global organizations help recognize where in the world the heaviest concentration of theme parks is located to study and support statistics about them. According to information obtained through these organizations, the most visited theme park group in the world is the Walt Disney attractions, based on number of guests in attendance over a one-year period, with Walt Disney World in Florida, USA taking the top spot as the most visited theme park in the world. Although Walt Disney attractions are often the first mentioned in conversations about theme parks, they are not the only ones advancing in their industry. Another front-runner is Universal Parks and Resorts, commonly referred to as Universal Theme Parks. It is a global competitor headquartered in Orlando, Florida, USA with four major theme parks located in Los Angeles, California, USA; Orlando, Florida, USA; Osaka, Japan; and Sentosa Island, Singapore. Future projects in the drafting or construction phase include theme parks in South Korea, Dubai, Moscow, and Beijing. Just as Disney takes its guests on a fully-themed adventure, Universal Theme Parks do the same, but focused on movies. The original park in Los Angeles, California is an actual movie set where guests can physically tour behind the scenes of movies with the chance to participate as extras! The experience created completely and most genuinely encompasses the experience-focused idea behind theme parks. While touring behind the scenes, guests can view sets of famous movies and, on occasion, witness films being shot. The rest of the park is designed to take them through the movie world with rides and attractions based on franchises such as Harry Potter, Fast and Furious, and Jurassic Park. These rides take them on a 3D adventure as if they were part of a movie. Guests experience a moment where they are 100% part of a fantasy world undistinguishable from reality during the attractions and rides, which is the exact desired outcome of their designers. And it is not just Disney and Universal offering these worlds of experiences to guests. There are equally impressive companies representing experience-focused attractions across the globe, created by the most innovative leaders in technology with unparalleled creativity.

Theme parks are attracting tourists from around the world to experience what they have to offer with all of these highly technological advances. And tourists are not the only ones they are attracting. The theme park industry has earned its place in the eye of the global economy. Companies are not the only ones participating directly in the parks, but cities and nations are as well. Local and world governments are beginning to recognize the financial effect these parks have on a destination, compelling them to partake more in these businesses. The travel and tourism sector is finally being acknowledged globally as a fierce competitor in the global economic game, and so accordingly, the theme park industry within that is proving to be a major asset to the sector and to destinations. In order for both of them to thrive, there must be a notable connection between a park and local tourism infrastructure. Just as local communities are affected by tourism, the theme park industry brings in a positive influence. Creating jobs is one of the biggest footprints of theme parks on local destinations. And often locations with theme parks bringing in guests have positive ripples into local hotels, restaurants, and smaller businesses surrounding the parks. The additional tourist spending in an area increases money funneled back into the community from the local government for improvements in transportation, facilities, as well as the overall infrastructure of the area.

Just as a destination can experience negative effects from an increase in tourist visits in general, the spike in tourist visits to a destination from theme parks can also carry a heavy weight. Local communities can best prepare and benefit from theme parks by accepting this new industry and niche of tourists. The theme park is unarguably a significant driver of the global economy, and when a destination is prepared for the increasingly large number of visitors these theme parks bring to its location, the theme park owners as well as the local communities and governments can reap positive rewards.

Part Six

The Future of Tourism

The travel and tourism industry began with the first flight of mankind, and has evolved into one of the top global economic powerhouses. At the rate the sector has grown, it will continue to grow to become the most innovative and progressive sector in the world because of technological advancements. With possibilities within reach for space tourism, the future of the tourist is bright. Developments are being made in every pocket of the industry. Like all successful business or industries, the tourism sector has constant attributes that carry it forward, as well as the necessary flexibility that will help it reach an even higher level of success. It is the seamless and fluid relationship of these two characteristics that make the tourism industry unique and unstoppable. Experts that are working around the clock to predict possibilities for the future help make it one of the most prepared sectors in the world for the future. Besides being on the brink of space tourism and future hotels, the sector is also embracing the beginnings of food tourism and sustainable tourism, recognizing their important potential for the future as well as their current priceless role in saving the future of the planet.

CONSTANTS

The phrase "history repeats itself" is relevant to more than just military and politics. It stems from the belief that similar events will repeat. Even though the tourism industry thrives on changing, innovative ideas, the reoccurrence of similar themes from the past creates the backbone of its future. These predictable intricacies have proven to be stable over time, and allow the sector to depend on certain constants. The roots of a business, industry, or even relationship are just as important as its hunger and drive for the future; the past often provides information that can unlock the answers for the days ahead. Simply put, the basic characteristics that make something tick are most genuinely the things that keep it going innately. The journey of the tourism industry began with the first steps of mankind and has been a living, growing thing since then, a sign that the industry has been doing something right. The constants that are believed to be universal in nature and in time, such as gravity, can be compared to the building blocks of any idea in the tourism field. Without taking into consideration the constant of gravity, ideas and formulas in physics would not work. And without respecting the proven successful constants in the tourism sector, future plans will be unpredictable.

There are two main constants in the tourism industry that help keep it consistent and stable. The first undeniable constant in the tourism industry is imagination. It is a key factor that drives not only the tourism business forward, but the tourist as well. The fluid exchange of ideas between industry leaders and the tourists themselves provides limitless innovative power that allows the industry the freedom to expand. Imagination is the power that separates the tourism industry from other industries and think outside the box to be constantly future-focused. Not many businesses, or sectors, push themselves to think so far into the future that it affects their decisions in the present. But in order for the sector to be successful, it must mitigate any problems that affect the industry, or any problems that arise as concerns for the future. And often enough the problems the sector faces are those of global concern like climate change or decreases in natural resources; these are problems the world is facing every day, but not every industry is addressing them because some think the problems won't directly affect them. While other industries ignore these serious problems, the tourism industry embraces addressing them in order to maintain destinations for the future and keep the industry thriving. If these issues are not addressed, the quality of the tourist's experience will decrease, leading to a decrease in visitors to destinations. The tourism industry is in fact helping to transform the world into a more sustainable planet. And none of that would be possible without imagination. Just like Disney's Imagineers thrust his business forward with futuristic thinking, the tourism industry does the same for itself. Imagination allows the sector to form ideas and scenarios in its mind about the future using current information and past occurrences. These thoughts help it make educated decisions, and apply its knowledge to solving future problems before they occur. Without imagination, the tourism industry would be a dying sector.

The second constant in the tourism sector is just as important as the first: the motivation for the tourist, the innate human need to continue traveling and exploring. As previously explored, this endless, hungry motivation has existed since the beginning of time, continues to compel tourists today, and will do the same into the future. Without this need and demand for travel, the industry simply would not exist because there would be no desire for its supply. This motivation has not only been unwavering, but has evolved and escalated century after century. People have become increasingly more interested in traveling and even more demanding in their expectations as travel and tourism have run on parallel lines. Innovation and technology push the tourist to reach further and want more.

Because of higher expectations from the tourist, the sector has been pushed to use its imagination to create better travel that it more innovative and exciting. It is a simple supply and demand, which is what really pushes most businesses forward. Without any expectations from guests or tourists, businesses would not bother to improve or exceed what is expected of them. But luckily, the tourism sector is serving mankind, whose innate passion for more and better is its number-one drive.

Without either one of these constants, the tourism sector would not be where it is today, nor would it be preparing for where it wants to be tomorrow. The sector's constants, like gravity, are responsible for the formation of the future; they are dependable building blocks upon which all other factors are built. The sector may be threatened by natural disasters and the depletion of resources, but these are the forces motivating the industry to address the future, instead of waiting for the collapse. In the face of destruction, the tourism industry is becoming the strongest sector in the world.

VARIABLES

It's not only the constants in the tourism industry that help it to exceed expectations. The changes that affect the future of tourism are just as important to the journey as the predictable backstory. Change itself is a constant, and there is no debate as to whether or not things change in the world. To evolve means to develop gradually, from a simple state to a more complex one. Again, the question is not if we are going to continue to evolve, but how fast will it happen and where it will lead. With change come variables. Although the tourism industry cannot embrace these variables and use them as they do with the known constants of its sector, it can continue to prepare itself for the possible future. In order to remain relevant, an industry or business must be able to change with the times. For example, if Motorola had not introduced the first mobile phone in the 1980s, where would they be today? Where would we be? Instead of continuing to produce the traditional telephone like all of the other phone companies, they stayed relevant, changed with the times, and anticipated and addressed the needs of the consumer. This act of reaching out beyond their current knowledge into the future helped them continue to be successful.

The main agents of change that will affect the future of tourism are technology and innovation, social structure, natural resources, and natural disasters. Technology and innovation are not only shaping the future of tourism, but the future of the world. Technology began with the conversion of natural resources into tools. The invention of the wheel pushed mankind forward with a quicker way to travel and control his environment. Technology is not restricted to machines or computers, but can refer to any innovation. In contemporary times, most technological advances relate to computers; machines; and devices and processes that help us to do something faster, smarter, or more user friendly. A lot of businesses, including the tourism sector, are heavily dependent on advances in technology.

Often when we imagine the future, we think of radical technological inventions that are hard to imagine ever being more than science fiction. Due to technological advances, they still seem possible. Before there were motion pictures in the nineteenth century, people did not think about the future as much; they didn't have any images of what the future could be, nor did they have any expectations of future inventions. Even with thousands of years of plays and stage performances, it was not until movies truly became accessible by everyone that science fiction became more prevalent. With this innovation came the churning minds of people expectant about the future. Motion pictures have become so advanced that any person who views them today has something of an expectation about the future. With all of the rapid technological advances of recent years, it is commonplace to think of a future that may appear to be science fiction, but will become reasonable. Companies are constantly providing real glimpses of what will be available such as gadgets, computers, robots, and even space hotels.

Mobile phones, robots, 3D images of people from across the globe, organs created from 3D machines to save patients were all once science fiction, and are now reality. In fact there is a high percentage of futuristic gadgets seen in science-fiction movies that have become real. If one paid attention closely to movies today, one would realize that most of them are prophecies. But instead of predictions that come from thin air, these come from an educated, forward-thinking group of people who can grasp the changes of the future now, even if only through media. But as technology continues to evolve, as the past shows us it will undoubtedly do, the tourism industry will change. The industry is dependent upon technology, whether in the form of future spacecrafts that will take tourists into orbit or the simple advances in user-friendly software that will aid in the planning of travel and exploring of far-off places at the touch of a button.

No one more important than another, all of the changes that will affect the future of tourism are intertwined. The world's social structure will be a big game changer for the industry as well. Global economic disorder will happen, but the details will be a surprise, as the future is still the future. But specialists and researchers have predicted that there will be a disorder unlike anything that has happened during our current days, which will shuffle the world order and trickle down to the social structure of nations, cities, and communities. These changes may affect tourism both positively and negatively, but most likely, evenly. Some nations will be thriving in new or accumulated wealth, offering their inhabitants the opportunities to travel the world with ease using newfound technology. Other nations will be thrown from pedestals into destruction both literally and economically, preventing their communities from traveling outside of their current locations. Although there are similar scenarios happening today, the future among nations holds even more drastic results that will affect the tourism industry.

The depletion of natural resources is something we are dealing with in today's world, which means the future of natural resources and their availability is already under threat. Natural resources are essential to our survival. They occur naturally in the environment, from which we extract them in order to live. Every single man-made item is essentially derived from a natural resource. Some natural resources such as water, air, and living organisms are consumed in their original, or natural, states. Other natural resources such as metal, oil, and most forms of energy need to be processed in order to be used. The depletion of these natural resources has already been identified, becoming a crux of the argument on how to use them responsibly. Many nations are in the business of exporting their local natural resources, causing even further concern about their depletion. Unfortunately, a majority of natural resources are considered to be finite, and without proper handling now, they will be depleted completely in the future. There are still a few resources that are considered inexhaustible such as sunlight, solar radiation, geothermal energy, and air. Although even with air, there is no guarantee that clean air for breathing safely will be accessible in the future. All of these resources, whether finite or inexhaustible, affect destinations of tourism. Places with an abundance of the resources can see a constant flow; tourists, and locals, may be driven away by a clear depletion of resources.

Natural resources tie into the tourism industry closer than most people are aware. The tourism industry is known to consume natural resources on a large scale. Often the level of visitor use of resources is greater than the destination's ability to cope with it. This in turn puts tremendous pressure on a location, leading to negative effects such as soil erosion, increased pollution, loss of natural habitats for wildlife, increased danger to endangered animals, and, most greatly, a strain on water resources. This struggle within the tourism industry directly affects the local community because they compete for the use of critical natural resources. Water resources are the number-one impact area on a local area from the tourism industry. Fresh water is the most critical natural resource on the planet, and the tourism sector is known for its overuse of water resources through hotels, swimming pools, golf courses, and personal use of tourists. This leads to water shortages and a degradation of water supplies. Tourism can also create pressure on a local destination's resources like food, energy, and raw materials. Land resources such as minerals, fossil fuels, fertile soil, wetlands, forests, and wildlife are also natural resources on which tourism takes a toll. The depletion of natural resources by the tourism industry is quite apparent, and threatening not just the industry but the planet. Without mindful choices now, salvaging the world's natural resources might prove to be impossible.

Changing climate patterns and natural disasters are connected. Destinations don't tend to rebound from natural disasters such as tsunamis or earthquakes. Developing countries known to depend more heavily on the tourism industry in comparison to developed countries are often hit harder, as disasters disrupt the economic structure as well as the physical disposition of the area. Even with disaster plans by businesses, governments, cities, and nations, it is predicted by scientists across the board that future climate changes and natural disasters will happen at a catastrophic level, quite possibly with the inability to recover from them. With this prediction on the table, the tourism industry on a global level may not be able to fully prepare for the future. But it's not impossible to prepare now, using educated predictions that could help battle these problems effectively.

SCENARIO PLANNING

In order to prepare for any situation, it's always better to have a plan, oftentimes more than one to take variables into account. In the tourism industry, the same idea is applied on a much larger scale. Scenarios are planned by nations, governments, organizations, and businesses with whatever knowledge and technology is available today to create solutions to the problems of tomorrow. It is a method used to make flexible long-term plans that take into consideration a variety of possibilities, solid facts based off history and current events, and alternate futures based off past events and educated opinions around a situation. Specialists use facts about demographics, geography, militaries, politics, and industry and take into consideration social, technical, economic, and environmental trends. The military as well as the political arena have been using this strategy for a long time. For example, policy makers use it to anticipate hidden weaknesses and inflexibilities in methods or organizations. One can imagine that most people base their decisions on information they currently possess and some sort of assumption of what the future could be, even if minutes or hours. In fact, people often use this forward-thinking method without even purposefully doing so. Imagine a business tourist preparing for an overseas vacation to a country he or she has never visited and about which he or she knows little. In packing and preparing, he or she might consider what possible scenarios into which he or she would run during the trip, based off of current knowledge and past experience. This type of thinking would force him or her to realize multiple possibilities for the future, and pack accordingly for all of them.

Scenario planning involves imagining scenarios that are both plausible and unexpected based off of problems that exist in some form today. While some scenarios of the future are easily grasped as possible, experts also consider situations that are both uncomfortable and almost unfathomable in order to push the planning to a level that would encourage functionality. With strategies being formed years in advance in some cases, weaknesses are addressed and avoided and their impact is reduced more effectively than if a situation were to come up as an unpredicted emergency situation. It is similar to how emergency medical professionals and emergency preparedness disaster workers prepare for the unexpected so that when the time arrives, they can rely on their knowledge and training for a situation, and are able to calmly move through it with the tools they have made available to themselves. It is simply smart business planning, and the tourism sector is on the cutting edge of it all.

Scenario planning is both a craft and a power on which the tourism sector has begun to capitalize, taking into consideration all of the changes that are happening now and predicted for the future that affect the industry's destinations and economic growth. In order to best utilize scenario planning to come up with all of the possible realities of the future, systems thinking is used, which is an organized way to approach complex situations by considering the many factors that create the future. Systematic thinkers for future planning are just like the systematic thinkers in tourism business management. They automatically use an all-inclusive method of analysis that concentrates on the way a system's fundamental segments interconnect, function over time, and perform within the bigger picture of even larger systems. This way of thinking is absolutely necessary in planning for the future. These researchers and thinkers have to also be able to embrace factors that are difficult to formalize, including insights about the future, dramatic shifts in values, and unprecedented regulations and inventions. Approaching the future with systems thinking through scenario planning is the most effective way to prepare for the future and all of its possibilities. Often a team made up of scientists, "Imagineers," and other professionals create the most effective and realistic scenarios about the future to prepare the world for what is to come. There are no predictions about the future that involve only one reality. Rather, by planning for a variety of possible futures, every possible outcome, and how to deal with each one, the world is better prepared than just by guessing. The scenarios become more plausible with the more variations that are presented, leading to effective planning for whatever the future brings.

The tourism sector battles with the variables that alter its state on a daily basis as well as the bigger, more advanced threats of the future. Like any successful manager, it is working to function on a high level in the present with the tourist in mind and embrace the future. By being concerned with a future that may be well beyond the years of the individuals now working in the sector, the tourism industry is going above and beyond what is expected of it. The tourism sector is in tune with the sustainability needs of the planet and how it intertwines with its needs for the future. The tourism sector is not only striving to be one of the top economic sectors in the world today, but is setting itself up to further excel as the top global industry. Although the industry keeps planning for the future to preserve the Earth and its sector, the predictive actions of the tourist are the real motivation. The tourist will continue to evolve with technology and want to travel more tomorrow than he or she does today. This is apparent and irreversible. History validates this prediction; mankind has had an increasing passion to travel. Future trends, technology, and scenario planning in the tourism sector will be connected closely to global planning to prevent future threats from collapsing the economy.

FUTURE TRENDS IN TOURISM

ECOTOURISM AND SUSTAINABLE TOURISM

Ecotourism and sustainable tourism are two of the most important, forward-thinking movements that will help to positively affect the future of the industry and the planet. In order for the world to continue thriving, it will require more than just the actions taken by the tourism sector. Environmentally- and socially-conscious travelers will be a key to making sure that travel is possible in the future. When it comes to the preservation of natural resources, these will be the people making that happen. With these trends already being put into motion today, their followers will have to push to make them mainstream living.

Ecotourism focuses on ecological conservation and educating tourists on travel that has minimal impact on the environment and the local community. It currently involves tourists visiting fragile and relatively undisturbed natural areas for their travels. It is a low-impact and small-scale alternative to the mass tourism and the heavily-trafficked locations of tourists and international commercial businesses. Moving forward, ecotourism will be linked more to spreading the word on the importance of this type of traveling in order to foster a respect for local communities, the planet, and its natural resources. Environmentalists have championed this endeavor as part of their commitment to the life of future generations and the preservation of destinations relatively untouched by human intervention. The future of ecotourism will be focused purely on maintaining and recruiting tourists to take up socially responsible travel, fostering an appreciation of natural habitats by avoiding conventional tourism avenues, and enhancing the integrity of the local communities. The movement to globally mainstream such actions as recycling, energy efficiency, and water conservation will be strongly pushed by ecotourists.

Sustainable tourism is an idea along the same lines as ecotourism in its goal to save the planet, but its intricacies vary. The goal of sustainable tourism is to make only positive impacts on the environment. Unlike ecotourism, which focuses on visiting only natural environments for their part in sustaining the world, sustainable tourism focuses on making a positive impact wherever tourists go. Tourism is highly dependent already on fossil fuels, and the industry has a heavy carbon footprint. Between transportation, accommodations, and local activities related to the tourism sector, the contribution to climate change is amplified far beyond the rest of the world. It is therefore an inherent responsibility that the tourism sector take action towards a positive, healthy future. The relationship between sustainable living and the tourism sector is strong; it is imperative that the sector, and tourists, be vigilant in sustainability. Without tourists, there is no travel and without sustainability practices, there are no destinations to which they can travel.

Sustainability is the attempt to reduce an individual's use of the Earth's natural resources and personal resources. By altering methods of eating, transportation, and energy consumption, all individuals, communities, and businesses can contribute to a sustainable future. Therefore, it is a type of tourism that can be taken up by everybody to wherever he or she travels. And the current movement in sustainable living is spreading across the globe. Sustainability is too big of an assignment and too much of a necessity to be taken on only by the tourism sector. But due to the severity of the depletion of the world's natural resources, and the sector's close relationship to that problem, the future of sustainable tourism is unavoidable. With the spread of tourists who want to make only a positive impact on the environment, society, and economy, the sector will have a helping hand in the movement for future sustainability. It is already a globally agreed-upon idea that all of tourism development moving forward should be sustainable. With this ideal, the trend of sustainability will become mainstream to benefit the future of tourism and restore the world.

FOOD TOURISM

Although food tourism may sound like merely the action of tourists eating while traveling, it reaches into a huge positive effect on our natural-resource supply and the tourism industry as a whole. Food tourism is quite simply the exploration of food as the purpose of travel. Food already ranks with climate, accommodation, and environment as being important to tourists. Food tourists are attracted often to the locally grown produce of a destination, which they see as deeply connecting them to the origins of a destination. Each destination becomes unique because of its offerings, which are appealing to the tourists who want to become part of the local community. Tourists today are seeking travel experiences based on local culture and identity, which revolve highly around food. A newer form of tourism, it is spreading widely across the globe as the food industry continues to explode through more and more restaurants and a growing industry of chefs and other careers.

But where is food tourism headed? Due to the changes in accessibility of organic food and the high trafficking of food across continents, food tourism is being forced in a different direction. The pursuit of a local food to its source is fighting against what another part of the food movement is trying to accomplish. In order to prepare the perfect plate or unique menu, professional and personal chefs and restaurateurs are importing raw ingredients that must travel hundreds and thousands of miles by land, air, or water across continents for the mere purpose of a single dish. With these unique products available with ease, food markets and grocery stores are partaking in this retrieval of food unique to distant locations in order to please their consumers. This trafficking of food across the globe is leaving a heavy carbon footprint, using up important, and limited, natural resources. This threatens the idea of food tourism and depletes natural resources quicker necessary to growing food. Another threat to food tourism is food waste. People in the gourmet food business who are determined to create the perfect menu or meal are not only importing local food from far-off destinations, but are wasting perfectly edible portions of produce, meat, and fish for presentation purposes. This is a widespread habit of those who are not directly affected by hunger. There are people who counter these chefs and businesses and go the extra mile to use only locally available food and repurpose every part of their food for consumption. The question is which foodie class weighs heavier than the other: the one that is depleting the natural food of the future at an accelerated rate for momentary pleasures or the group that understands sustainability and its important future? The tourism industry must take both into consideration for the future because they each leave their own mark on the environment.

Either way, food tourism is evolving, and is predicted to continue changing into the future. There are multiple possibilities for how it will end up depending on the popularity of people living sustainable lifestyles versus that of those contributing to a faster depletion of natural resources. If the scale tips towards the part of humankind that is environmentally aware, then the future of tourism will lean toward one future. And if the depletion of natural resources happens faster than anticipated, then a complete collapse is more likely.

Besides man, science will be a determinant of the future of food tourism. There is the possibility that food tourism will continue to seek out food grown naturally from the Earth at every destination. But the parallel future may be an elevated version of today's obsession with master chefs with artificially created cuisines. Scientists have been creating synthetic food for mankind in preparation as a solution for possible future food shortages. Unlike genetically modified organisms (GMO) that splice in traits from other species to create the food we see on the shelves of markets today, synthetic biology involves the creation of new organisms in a lab with their own full DNA. The technology used to do this is closely guarded to prevent an adverse reaction from the public of anxiety and distrust. But in order for the planet, and food tourism, to flourish in the future, all possible outcomes must be explored and prepared. If synthetic food is the future, food tourism may focus more on the technology used to create these foods and the unique outcomes it might explore. Some may scour the planet still in search of natural food, as it becomes a rare and much desired delicacy. In fact, the pursuit of organic, natural food for tourism purposes may become reserved for the wealthy class and unattainable to the rest of the world. But just because synthetic food is undesirable to the world today, the burden of the predicting the future of how to feed the world in the face of depleted resources has been taken up responsibly by scientists through extensive, and reliable, scenario planning.

SPACE TOURISM

Space Tourism. The phrase itself sounds very futuristic to most. But space travel has been around for many decades with astronauts, known as space tourists, having been out and about in the universe since the first human spaceflight in 1961. But space tourism doesn't just refer to space science and space exploration. Space tourism deals more specifically with everyday human traveling into space for leisure, business, or recreational purposes. Although it may not be everybody's reality, it is for some. We mostly hear about space travel when astronauts take a journey into the beyond, but there are many space tourism companies that exist today that have taken individuals into space for leisure. Since 2007, there have been multiple companies promising space tourism and selling space rides to individuals across the globe, but only a small portion have delivered the service. Although this sounds like science fiction to most people today, with the amount of companies focusing on the space tourism industry it is only a matter of time before the trend becomes mainstream. This could quite possibly emerge overnight. Although orbital space tourism is limited and extremely expensive, it does exist. A small amount of ordinary people have already orbited just more than 100 kilometers above the Earth's atmosphere, which is the official U.S. definition of what makes an astronaut. But with few trips complete, and with lives lost attempting the journeys, space tourism has yet to become conventional, even to the wealthiest. But most experts surmise that once short trips outside the Earth's atmosphere become regularly available because of the research in space travel by space scientists, the possibilities for the future will erupt.

Planning for the future of space travel is happening across the globe. The ability for space travel as common as a flight across the sea is at the fingertips of mankind. The two big categories of space tourism are to secure life on another planet in order to preserve mankind to counter the depletion of resources and collapse of society and the space travel that will be available to all of mankind like any other destination on Earth. Just as travel across the world has become more and more accessible to all classes of people with the advancement of technology, experts presume that space travel will do the same. As it becomes more prevalent, hotels may be built in space, and over time it will become just another destination choice to consider for a holiday.

Imagine planning a holiday for a weekend getaway. Your motivation is to completely relax and find a destination where your daily stresses melt away until they seem insignificant. You would love to be able to completely let go of it all and enjoy some tranquil views from your hotel. While flipping through travel sites on the Internet, you come across a special on a weekend space package. A flight that would take only ten minutes could propel you just outside the Earth's atmosphere. From there, you would have a quick transfer to one of many space hotels. You are weightless there, shedding all the heavy burdens on your life. While orbiting the Earth every ninety minutes, you would be able to experience not only a magnificent view of Earth, but one filled with more than fifteen sunsets and sunrises. A truly transcendent experience to bring back to Earth days later. The possibilities for the future are infinite. Experts predict that trips outside the Earth's orbit to the moon or destination space hotels are within reach to our current young generations. Space travel, along with Walt Disney, has proven that if you can imagine it, it is possible.

THE FUTURE TOURIST

We know who the first tourists were, what they wanted, and all of the current motivations for tourists and types of travel. But who are the future tourists? Will they all be space tourists clamoring to travel beyond Earth's atmosphere? Or like today, will most enjoy the respite of casual travel within their reach by car, train, boat, or airplane? There are some guarantees of what the future tourist will be like. If early mankind didn't have a need to move materials and belongings from one place to another more quickly, then the wheels of a car would not exist. If it weren't for the innovations of the Wright Brothers, then there would be no flight, no planes, and no quick journeys across seas. The ideas and inventions of today's scientists, inventors, engineers, Imagineers, and creators begin to form the future of tourism. History repeats itself. There are always people inventing gadgets and surmising theories that seem impossible, irrational, and often ridiculous. And from them have come every single great invention in history! The future tourist will be a product of the labors of the inventors of today. *We* will form that future tourist. We will create a myriad of possibilities, all a little out of reach today, that the future tourist will fill eventually.

And it will not just be space flight. Jet planes will replace the hefty airplanes of today's airline companies, whisking people across continents possibly only for a meal or a party instead of a long-planned trip in a fraction of the time it takes today. Holidays will include weekend getaways to foreign lands at the same relative price of a local hotel resort today. The motivation for travel was ignited in the first community of mankind and has not lost momentum. The same will be true of the future tourist. He or she will have the same motivation that moves mankind away from its familiar surroundings and out into the unknown. The differences between the tourist today and the future tourist are the same as those between the cave man and current man. Innovation. Technology. The future tourist will be in line with the technology of his or her time and the innovations that allow him or her to move. That tourist will not have the same technology as the tourist today. He or she will be further advanced technologically. Destinations and attractions will also change. The future scenario the Earth is fated for will determine the environments and destinations available to the future tourist. Scenario planning allows us to predict multiple futures for the tourist. And with the educated options produced today, we can presume that the future tourist will fit perfectly into one of them.

Experts can agree that the future holds many unknowns. But at the same time, the inventions experts are creating today will only enhance the future. Whether the technology enhances the problems and brokenness of society or enhances solutions for the already capable humankind, the future is being built today. But when it comes down to it, a tourist wants more. He or she wants to explore and to enhance his or her spiritual, physical, and emotional self.

We are all tourists searching for something else, something better, and something different. If nothing else has come from this book, it is that each and every one of us is a tourist. At one time or another, we have all been internally pushed away from our familiar surroundings to another location or externally tugged at to go somewhere else. Whether you have traveled only miles from your home to visit family or have been one of the few to leave Earth's orbit: You are a tourist. Every person since the beginning of time has been, and all of mankind moving forward will be. If there is one definite about the future, is it that all of us and our future generations will freely be the tourists we are motivated to be.

www.ingramcontent.com/pod-product-compliance
Lightning Source LLC
LaVergne TN
LVHW051556080426
835510LV00020B/3000
* 9 7 8 0 6 9 2 7 0 4 2 1 9 *